SAY YES TO NO DEBT

"I knew Dr. Soaries had a reputation for being an incredible preacher. But to walk into his church is to feel the power of a man who professes to do more than just interpret the Bible — he preaches of profound personal transformation. His battle moves the church beyond the struggles of segregation and Jim Crow, to a place where it empowers individuals to change the future for everyone."

— SOLEDAD O'BRIEN, television journalist

"Dr. Soaries' unique background has prepared him for impactful ministry. This book skillfully illustrates that biblical principles, when applied to our lives, make for practical solutions to everyday challenges. And the area of finances is no different. The church has the message in Scripture. I thank God for using Buster to give us another strategy for spreading that message."

— DR. ANTHONY EVANS, senior pastor, Oak Cliff Bible
    Fellowship, president, The Urban Alternative

"In an age of 'feel good' messages and strategies, 'Buster' Soaries exits the road to 'easy street' and invites individuals, churches, ministries, and families to enter the on-ramp to debt-free living. Buster exposes the heart issue associated with an over-consumption lifestyle, and from there he shines a beautiful, practical, and biblical light on the liberation that comes when we unlock the handcuffs of debt. I'm personally a student, a believer, and a soul set free."

— DAN WOLGEMUTH, president/CEO, Youth for Christ/USA

"Dr. DeForest Soaries is a gift to the body of Christ and to everyone who desires to be out of financial bondage. Debt keeps a majority of us bound. We cannot be spiritually free and in financial debt. dfree® not only enables us to handle money God's way, it also enables us to be and live the life God desires for us. I endorse and encourage everyone to get, read, and embrace what the book teaches."

— BISHOP REGINALD T. JACKSON,
African Methodist Episcopal Church

"Over the years, I have watched Dr. Soaries courageously tackle some of the more challenging issues of our time. Again, when the economy crumbled, and the housing dreams of so many with it and foreclosures mounted, Soaries and his church responded. Talk is cheap. ... He was given yet another dream and vision to help rebuild lives through their debt-free, recovery program. The entire community rejoices in his fine work!"

— DONALD HILLIARD JR., DMin, senior pastor,
Cathedral International

"Having known my brother 'Buster' all of my life, I can honestly say he genuinely cares about the financial well-being and economic soundness of those around him. He is a born leader and seeks to empower other leaders to demonstrate care through action. Debt-free living is not really an option. It is a biblical command to 'owe no man' (Romans 13:8). In our complex, modern, social, and economic systems, this seems impossible, but this book reveals otherwise. This must-read book provides a key to breaking free from the myth that creating, accepting, and living in continual debt is the path to wealth and happiness. Instead, it realistically and honestly guides the reader into the truth regarding debt-free living and a life free from the stress of financial mismanagement."

— DR. CRAIG E. SOARIES, founder and pastor,
Global Empowerment Center

"*Say Yes to No Debt: 12 Steps to Financial Freedom* is exactly what people need to get their finances on track. As a church member who conducts financial seminars at my home church, I am thrilled that there is a resource that I can point fellow members to that will give them a practical guide to using God's principles to banish debt from their lives and get on a path to true financial freedom."

    — LISA WARNER PICKRUM, CEO, The RLJ Companies,
       member, Largo Community Church

"It is my joy to endorse such a relevant and timely book. Rev. DeForest B. Soaries, Jr. has gained a national reputation as a pastor who has a shepherd's heart. This well-earned reputation is powerfully reinforced by this book. In a season where so many are suffering economically, he shares with the reader step-by-step solutions in dealing with and avoiding unnecessary debt. This work deserves a hearty 'Amen!'"

    — BISHOP JOHN R. BRYANT, presiding prelate senior bishop,
       African Methodist Episcopal Church

"In Revelation 1:11, John is told, 'What thou seest write in a book.' My friend and brother Dr. 'Buster' Soaries has, with courage, clarity, and conviction, put pen to paper and, with prophetic tone, confronted the church and community with this powerful message. Because Dr. Soaries 'saw' the danger of debt, he led his people at First Baptist Church of Lincoln Gardens on a brave journey to debt-free living. I strongly recommend dfree® to anyone who desires to destroy, drop, or be delivered from debt. This book will change your thinking, your habits — it will change your life."

    — BISHOP TIMOTHY J. CLARKE, senior pastor,
       First Church of God

"With keen theological insight, Dr. Soaries, an able preacher and pastor, places our financial resources within the context of our responsibility as people of God to be good stewards of the resources He has entrusted to us, recognizing the timeless biblical truth that 'The earth is the Lord's' (Psalm 24:1). In a consumer-oriented age, this book will help both the church and individuals free themselves from the slavery of debt, delinquency, and deficits that invariably hinder the purposes, plan, and call of God's kingdom."

— Rev. Dr. J. Wendell Mapson Jr., pastor,
Monumental Baptist Church

"In times of severe economic shortfalls, Dr. Soaries has written a timely, insightful, relevant manual for the twenty-first-century church and its leadership. It's a must read for every pastor who desires to lead their congregation toward solid financial stewardship. Soaries takes economic justice into a practical, demonstrative new-think."

— Rev. Gerald Lamont Thomas, PhD, Senior Pastor,
Shiloh Baptist Church

"When I first moved to New Jersey in 1995, I sought a church — a place my family and I could call home and look to for guidance. I was most impressed by Reverend Soaries. He cared not just about our lives on Sunday morning, but was wholeheartedly involved in the entire community Monday through Saturday. During the Imus controversy with the Rutgers women's basketball team in 2007, it was Pastor Soaries who helped us to stand tall. He will always be my inspiration."

— C. Vivian Stringer, Rutgers University
women's basketball head coach, 2009 Inductee,
Naismith Memorial Basketball Hall of Fame

"DeForest Soaries' embarking upon this mission called dfree®, aided by the writing of this book, is a natural outcome of his many years of passion for serving and aiding people in discovering the better possibilities for life and living. Having had the privilege of knowing, sharing, and working with Buster in many capacities for forty years, I consider it an awesome challenge keeping up with his level of fervor for serving his fellow man. That being said, this book is a natural as it represents his desire to share, beyond his congregation, with 'whosoever will,' the way to live beyond 'debt, delinquencies, and deficits.'"

> — CALVIN MCKINNEY, pastor, Calvary Baptist Church
> of North Jersey at Garfield; General Secretary,
> National Baptist Convention, USA, Inc.

"DeForest B. Soaries is a genius. With creative ingenuity, he has developed a plan and a process to liberate individuals, the church and community from financial instability to a life of prosperity. Anyone who is willing to take a leap of faith, and follow the dfree® plan will create a whole new existence for themselves. It will work if you work it!"

> — REV. DR. CYNTHIA L. HALE, senior pastor,
> Ray of Hope Christian Church

"Pastor DeForest 'Buster' Soaries, Jr's dfree® concept is the answer to the debt question millions are grappling with. This book is absolutely amazing and will unlock the prison of financial bondage that has devastated so many lives. I have heard testimony after testimony of the success of dfree®. This book is a must read."

> — DR. TERESA HAIRSTON, founder/publisher,
> *Gospel Today* magazine

I am so grateful that Dr. Soaries has written a book that speaks to our culture. Most financial books just provide financial literacy, but Dr. Soaries gets to the root of our spending by dealing with the psychological and emotional spending habits of individuals. *Say Yes to No Debt* provides a roadmap to skillful stewardship. The emancipation from college loans, credit card debt, and medical bills can truly set financial captives free.

— DR. DARRYL K. WEBSTER, Emmanuel Missionary Baptist Church, Indianapolis, Indiana

Pastor Soaries is well qualified to write a book on the work he has been doing most of his life. He 'walks the talk,' which is becoming rare today. He is a teacher and a scholar.

— STEDMAN GRAHAM, businessman, author, speaker

To rid yourself of the shackles of debt, you must first get your mind right. *Say Yes to No Debt* is the perfect book to help you do just that, by unpacking the psychological causes behind debt and then offering insightful, yet highly practical strategies for debt-free living. But *Say Yes to No Debt* is more than a book, or even just a concept. It's a movement that can help Americans of all backgrounds and faiths.

— LYNNETTE KHALFANI-COX, The Money Coach® and author of *The New York Times* bestseller *Zero Debt: The Ultimate Guide to Financial Freedom*

SAY YES TO NO DEBT

SAY YES TO NO DEBT

12 STEPS
TO FINANCIAL FREEDOM

DeForest B. Soaries, Jr.

Previously titled
dfree™: Breaking Free from Financial Slavery

ZONDERVAN

Say Yes to No Debt
Copyright © 2011, 2015 by DeForest B. Soaries Jr.

Previously published as dfree™: Breaking Free from Financial Slavery

Requests for information should be addressed to:
Zondervan, 3900 Sparks Dr. SE, Grand Rapids, Michigan 49546

ISBN 978-0-310-34396-7 (softcover)

ISBN 978-0-310-34397-4 (ebook)

Cover photography: Joel Benard, Masterfile®
Interior design: Beth Shagene

First printing September 2015 / Printed in the United States of America

To the memories of my two grandmothers

Mary E. Pinkard
and
Carrie L. Soaries

Contents

Level III – Get Ahead

Level IV – Give Back

Introduction

Consumer Debt — The New Slavery

The borrower is slave to the lender.

Proverbs 22:7

IMAGINE STROLLING THROUGH THE GROCERY STORE AND SUDdenly noticing that most of the other shoppers are wearing chains around their wrists and ankles. The new mother with her little girl sitting in the front of the cart. The older gentleman contemplating brands of breakfast cereal. The college student reaching for the frozen pizza. The career woman grabbing dinner for her family on the way home from work. All of them seemingly oblivious to the weighty encumbrance of heavy iron chains securing their arms and legs.

Then you begin to notice that most people are shackled wherever you go. Standing in line for tickets at the movie theater, or walking down the hall at work, or welcoming people into the foyer at church, you see the same powerful chains binding the limbs of those around you. Everyone smiles and nods — "How are you today?" "Oh, I'm fine, and you?" — working hard to ignore the debilitating burden that so limits their movements. Many seem to pretend that the chains aren't even there, while others adjust them as if they were new accessories from the jewelry store. You wonder if you're dreaming or watching a new science fiction program on TV, when you look down and see the same enormous iron chains gripping your own hands and feet.

Such a disturbing spectacle would be hard to ignore, particularly if no one else seemed to notice or to be troubled by it. The passive acceptance of such enslavement would seem particularly surprising in a country that upholds human freedom as a cornerstone value — freedom of speech, freedom of religion, and freedom to vote for whomever we choose. However, such enslavement does bind many of us and inhibits our freedom every day. While invisible to the naked eye, heavy chains of consumer debt are squeezing life out of millions of Americans right now.

Perhaps the most stunning fact is that our twenty-first-century slavery is self-imposed and self-perpetuated. Hundreds of years ago, men and women were ambushed and violently captured against their will, literally dragged thousands of miles away from their homeland and forced into hard labor that often cost them their lives. Today, men and women are ambushed by their own poor choices, impulse purchases, and attempts to keep up with a mirage-like cultural standard of consumer consumption. They remain shackled by high interest rates and low minimum payments. Men and women today resign themselves to a desperate, hopeless future in which they can never dig out of their financial pit.

Plastic Shackles

Consumer debt grips millions of people with plastic shackles every bit as powerful as the iron chains that once bound slaves. A bold, even audacious, statement, I know, particularly considering the historical atrocities of slavery in our country. As a descendant of some of those slaves, I do not make this analogy without recognizing the gravity of its implications. I do not make such a comparison lightly or for the sheer effect of its cultural shock value, although the ongoing enslavement of millions of Americans should shock and concern all of us. While many of my fellow African Americans may be particularly upset or offended by my literal comparison, I find that *enslavement* is the only adequate word to express the dire, life-draining, debilitating condition in which we find ourselves today.

When I shared my view for a recent CNN documentary on debt among African Americans, Soledad O'Brien, my interviewer, did a double take and asked if I was sure of my assertion. Without hesitation, I confirmed my statement with a resounding "yes." I repeated the message that has become my mantra over the last few years: Consumer debt enslaves millions of people in our country with debilitating chains that only seem to grow tighter each month as bills increase and income decreases. We've shackled ourselves with fear, stress, and shame by spending far more than we're taking in or saving. However, the time has come to emancipate ourselves. That's what this book — and dfree® living — is all about: your financial *freedom*.

You may be wondering how I know what I'm talking about. Granted, I'm not an expert accountant or financial guru, but I know firsthand the harsh realities of economic imprisonment. As the pastor of a large suburban church in New Jersey, I've shared in the many struggles of my members — unemployment, unpaid bills, depleted retirement accounts, and foreclosed mortgages. As a government official and community development leader, I've similarly experienced the impact of layoffs, shrinking budgets, and corporate bankruptcy. And as a middle-class American who was once seduced by easy credit and then overwhelmed by staggering balances, I've waged my own personal battle for fiscal freedom.

Foremost, I've learned that overwhelming debt exists and continues to grow in every sector of American life across every demographic — gender, race, education level, and pay scale. No one is immune, not bankers, teachers, executives, accountants, artists, or entrepreneurs. Not only is our nation drowning in debt but many American citizens have also become addicted to a lifestyle that perpetuates the use of credit cards, high-interest loans, and borrowing against future earnings. This problem had escalated to epidemic proportions long before the Great Recession of 2008 officially identified our crisis. The Center for American Progress reported in July 2006 that 56 percent of blacks, 42 percent of Hispanics, and 46 percent of whites considered their debt levels a serious problem.

So even after our most recent economic downturn, we persist in growing our consumer debt, which is rising faster than our incomes. Based on data from the Federal Reserve and other government agencies:

- The size of the total consumer debt in the U.S. grew nearly five times in size from 1980 ($355 billion) to 2001 ($1.7 trillion). As of October 2014, consumer debt totaled $3.23 trillion.

- The average household in December 2014 carried nearly $15,611 in credit card debt.

- According to the U.S. Census Bureau, by December 2013 133 million households in the United States had $875 billion in revolving credit (primarily credit cards).

- According to the Federal Reserve, in 2014, 71% of Americans have credit cards; 33% have one to two; 18% have three to four; 9% have five to six; 7% have seven credit cards or more.

- According to the National Foundation for Credit Counseling, 7% of Americans were rejected for a new credit card in 2014, up from 4% in 2011.

Despite having recently come through the Great Recession of 2008, the national hole of debt continues as a reality in our culture. The National Foundation for Credit Counseling reported in its "2014 Consumer Financial Literacy Survey" that approximately 24% of Americans acknowledged that they weren't paying all their bills on time and 24% also report having no savings at all.

We've come to accept, as normal, a lifestyle in which we are always behind, borrowing from our future earnings to assuage our present bill collectors to pay for a forgotten past. It has become so normal that, as of 2014, Americans have more than two trillion dollars' worth of consumer debt. Two *trillion* dollars — that's twelve zeroes! Owing trillions of dollars, we now face banks that are finally realizing that consumers have borrowed more money than they can afford to pay back. Many lenders have already lost more money on unpaid credit card debt than they did on defaulted mortgage loans. Some experts predict that 10 percent of that consumer debt will never be repaid.

A Spiritual Solution

These staggering statistics beg a larger question than "How did this happen?" No, we must ask ourselves a harder question: *What's wrong with us?* How did we become a nation of people who, across ethnic backgrounds, religious beliefs, income brackets, and educational levels, have fallen prey to the temptation of spending more money than we have? What caused us to become a people who are more likely to spend our money before we earn it?

This pattern of widespread behavior is historically unprecedented. How did we get a whole nation of people to say, "I would rather pay high interest rates than wait until I can afford to buy what I need"? Many experts fear that the residential mortgage crisis that triggered a global meltdown a few years ago is just the tip of the economic iceberg. The mortgage crisis is not the problem; it's just an example of the problem. The real problem is within us, and I'm convinced its only solution is spiritual.

Before you're tempted to dismiss my conviction that overspending is a spiritual problem with a spiritual solution, let me share a startling piece of data. In a twelve-month period during the height of our recent recession, during a time when almost every charity, ministry, philanthropy, and church saw donations plummet, my church's giving *increased* by more than a million dollars!

And it had nothing to do with my skills as a fundraiser or my ability to browbeat members into tithing more. In fact, much to my church board's initial dismay, I refused to make fundraising central to my pastoral role or to give guilt-inducing sermons on tithing. Instead, I focused my teaching on the freedom of debt-free living and developed a movement that we came to call "dfree®."

My inspiration for our approach came out of a desperate situation. In 2003, at the conclusion of a church building campaign that exceeded a decade of planning and a cost of $20 million, the First Baptist Church of Lincoln Gardens, New Jersey, found itself with a multi-million-dollar mortgage and dwindling funds. While overall giving had increased steadily by at least 10 percent in each year of my tenure, the church resources had been drained by over-budget construction costs and unexpected litigation to get the job finished.

Something had to change, and the sooner the better, if we were going to survive the financial tsunami racing toward our shore. During one of many meetings to brainstorm solutions, I found myself on the hot seat. As the trustees and church leaders looked to me, as senior pastor, for a solution, someone suggested that I preach more sermons about tithing.

In fact, the person who made the suggestion stated that they had never heard me preach an entire sermon focused exclusively on tithing. With a sound rationale, this person explained that the church's problem resulted from members who were not giving at least 10 percent of their income, and therefore our solution was simply for these people to be motivated, encouraged, cajoled, and challenged to do so — a responsibility that, they all assumed, fell under my job description.

Many other board members agreed with this logic. They had done the math and concluded that if our 4,000 members all gave 10 percent of their salaries as their tithe, we would be in great financial shape. And they expected, almost demanded, that I, as their pastor, make it happen. Feeling a bit queasy, I left the meeting with a commitment to get back to them soon with my response to their recommendation.

Driven to dfree®

I was at a crossroads. At that point I had been there for fifteen years and had accomplished the big task the church wanted me to lead them in completing: their new building. Maybe it was the perfect time for me to transition out of leadership at First Baptist and make room for a successor who could come and preach as many sermons on tithing as they wanted. And please understand: I'm certainly not against tithing and will discuss it in more detail later in the book. But I was uncomfortable concluding that tithing was a solution to the church's financial pressures. I would have to seek God's guidance like never before.

After much prayer and focused concentration on my ministry, I went to the church on Saturday for an event. For some reason the cars in the parking lot grabbed my attention and somehow looked different than I'd ever seen them before. I was used to finding a full parking lot before a service or event, but I'd never really noticed the cars that people drove to church. However, on this Saturday I noticed that our parking lot was virtually a luxury car showroom. Our members were driving the finest cars made, leaving my reliable Ford Expedition (which I bought at a great price from my cousin who owned a dealership) in the dust. Sedans, SUVs, and sports cars made by Mercedes Benz, BMW, Lincoln, and Cadillac lined up beside each other — I even saw a Maserati!

What was going on? The parking lot of a church straining to pay its bills on time was full of high-end luxury cars? At that moment, the reality of the situation sparkled like sunlight off the chrome of the convertible next to me. Suddenly, it seemed clear that I was getting the directional insight I so desperately needed. Our members were driving late-model luxury cars, wearing beautiful designer clothes, taking exotic vacations, and dining in the best restaurants. But could they really *afford* such lavish lifestyles?

It seemed more likely that they were borrowing money at high finance rates to buy those cars and using high-interest credit cards to purchase everything else. My answer was right there: *our people could not give more to the church because they did not have it to give.* Before they even received their paychecks, their money was spent — instantly consumed by bills, credit cards, mortgages or rent, and car payments.

My revelation was clear: If the church helped the people get out of debt, then the people would naturally — without being pressured — help the church get out of debt. We would launch a churchwide campaign to attack the culture of debt and deficit living. Within days, I shared my vision with the trustees, and one caught it right away. He and his wife had been our church's largest financial supporters, and he immediately saw the big picture. This man had a passion to teach people biblical principles about money, and this was definitely the direction he believed the church should take.

His encouragement was all I needed — and for a while it was all I received. The others had a more "wait and see" attitude. But I knew that this was the direction God wanted the church to take, and I also knew that I had to stay there to lead the strategy. As we brainstormed names for this new movement, I focused on the issues we wanted to combat: using credit excessively, struggling under high-interest rates, and living above our means.

Three words popped into my mind to encapsulate these challenges: debt, delinquency, and deficit. However, I didn't want to focus the program on the problem when we could name the solution. And the solution is freedom — freedom from debt, freedom from delinquency, and freedom from deficit. So the name for our program became "dfree®"!

During the months and years that followed, we experienced both tremendous resistance and enormous rewards with the dfree® program at First Baptist, and I'll share some of them throughout the book. Bottom line, we became a congregation of people committed to overcoming our individual financial problems with a community approach that included education, accountability, encouragement, and evangelism — spreading the good news that God sets us free in every area of our lives, including our slavery to consumer debt.

As enthusiasm translated into action, our church's income rose accordingly — with no sermons on tithing whatsoever! After six months of the dfree® campaign, the church's income rose by $500,000. By the end of the first twelve months of dfree® at First Baptist, our income increased by a million dollars! More than six hundred households were exposed to some level of dfree® instruction in the first years, and the message became and remains a part of the entire church culture.

Emancipation Proclamation

Today dfree® has evolved into a large-scale movement that has successfully liberated thousands of people. While its primary growth has been nourished by the community support of our church, the core principles of dfree® apply to anyone longing to release themselves from the shackles of their financial slavery. Regardless of setting, the focus remains on educating, motivating, and activating individuals to live in complete freedom.

You don't need to be part of a group, church, or institution to implement the dfree® strategy and experience the liberating joy of a debt-free life. As we'll discuss later, finding a community committed to dfree® living is crucial for your success. But this community can develop from your existing network of family, friends, colleagues, and other like-minded individuals who are willing to support, encourage, and inspire you on your path to freedom.

Nor do you need specialized business knowledge or a passion for accounting. The solution to our dilemma is not more information. Hundreds of books have been written by financial experts more qualified than I on the fundamentals of finances. If it were simply a matter of education, then none of us would be enslaved to debt. If losing weight were as simple as learning to eat healthy food and exercise more, then no one would be obese. We all know there are plenty of diet books, nutritional regimens, and exercise routines that would help us lose weight, improve our health, and feel better. So why aren't we doing it?

For the same reasons, we remain resigned to financial slavery. Like someone imprisoned for so long that he resists walking away even after he's been handed the key, most of us know what we need to do but remain stuck, paralyzed by fear, anger, stress, shame, and denial. Instead, we need a strategy that addresses the emotional, cultural, psychological, and spiritual causes of self-destructive spending. My hope is that this book can become your personal emancipation proclamation from financial slavery.

If you want to reclaim your freedom and leave the shackles of debt behind, then dfree® provides this comprehensive strategy. Anchored by the wisdom of God's Word, the dfree® process of liberation focuses on four levels:

Get Started. Unless we admit the problem, we will never be free. The goal in this first level is to introduce you to the basics of reclaiming financial responsibility as the key to freedom. By facing the full reality of your financial "dis-ease," you can gain an objective perspective on how your problem has snowballed and how to change course. When you admit the problem and assess your current status, you've then paved the way for changing your attitude, the ultimate crucial step in level one.

Get Control. In level two, the goal is to develop a spending plan that actually reflects your current reality as well as the financial freedom you long to experience. This process involves taking action and changing habits and lifestyle patterns to support your new top-priority goal of financial freedom. With a dfree® time line in place, participants can enjoy achieving the smaller goals that contribute to their ultimate objective.

Get Ahead. This level focuses on achieving the basic goals of your spending plan and maintaining fiscal health through savings, investments, and real estate. As you begin to get your financial house in order, you must protect your assets, make investment decisions, and enhance long-term strategies. Once you've established the basics, it's important to make sure your future is secure through retirement and estate planning, including health and life insurance.

Give Back. The final level completes the process of dfree® living and celebrates the joy of financial freedom. Investing your resources of money, time, and possessions allows you to experience the true bounty of your riches and to share them with others. Many people at this level mentor others, teach dfree® principles to groups, or ignite the dfree® movement at their church.

Financial freedom does not happen accidentally or overnight; it happens as the cumulative effect of consistent, deliberate decisions we make each day. While knowing the facts about a problem helps us understand its origin, rarely is the solution simply a matter of mastering the data. Much of our behavior and many of our decisions have little to do with facts.

We make decisions based on what others are doing or what others may think; we make decisions based on our own feelings; we make decisions based on past experiences; we make decisions based on perceived expectations; and we make reactionary decisions to avoid pain, disappointment, and discomfort. Our money and issues involving our personal finances are especially charged with emotional and psychological baggage.

The success of dfree® is based on our ability to recognize and tap into the reality of why we've made the fiscal decisions we've made and to help us make healthy financial decisions using our insight into our own decision-making process. By creating a critical mass of financially healthy behavior, we discover the immense freedom and unfettered joy that come from debt-free living. We discover how to use the resources with which we're entrusted to serve God's purposes and not merely our own gratification.

Consumer debt is slavery. Lasting freedom is available. If you want to be free, my friend, if you want to say yes to no debt, then take the first step and turn the page.

Get

STARTED

"My wife and I are both college educated, with good jobs, two cars, and a nice home. With four kids, two older and two younger, we have always used our credit cards to get by when something comes up. While we've known a lot of the basic financial information before, it didn't hit home until I lost my job due to a corporate downsizing and began to panic when I realized just how deep in consumer debt we had fallen. It felt like the weight of the world had fallen on my shoulders all at once.

"I discovered dfree® through a friend who was familiar with the movement at Pastor Soaries' church in New Jersey. When I asked my friend what was different about dfree® from other financial programs or methods, he said that it got to the heart of the problem, not just the symptoms. This intrigued me, and I have to say that my friend is right.

"A lot of the reasons why we had become so dependent on credit cards had nothing to do with money. We were trying to keep up with a standard of living that doesn't reflect our values or who we really are. I was fortunate to find another job fairly fast, and it even paid a little better than the one I lost. But how we approached our finances had changed for good.

"I'm happy to say that we're now on the road to being debt-free, thanks to the principles of dfree®. For the first time in years, I don't dread paying the bills each month. The hardest part was getting started, but once you take the first step, then you can take another, and another, and soon you're on your way to a debt-free life."

Doug S., Denver, Colorado

1

Admit the Problem

Coming to Your Senses,
Acknowledging Slavery

IMAGINE IF VISA OR MASTERCARD SENT ME THE FOLLOWING letter: "Dear Mr. Soaries, We're pleased to send you a brand-new credit card. It's still going to carry platinum privileges, but we're changing the name from *Platinum* to *Slave*. We know you'll enjoy using your new Slave Card. The best card you can have. *Slave.*"

You get my point. Financial institutions don't send us "slave cards"; they send out gold or platinum cards. They would never use the term *slave* in any reference, and we would be understandably offended if they did. Instead we proudly whip out our gold card and hand it over to the cashier as if we're extra special instead of especially enslaved.

The first step for getting out of slavery must be *identifying the reality of our condition*. We must acknowledge that the truth of Proverbs applies to us: "The borrower is servant to the lender" (22:7b). The word translated as "servant" can also be accurately rendered as "slave." And the reality of our condition is that we are servants or slaves to our lenders. With this admission as our starting point, we can then begin to break the stranglehold of debt with a three-tiered approach.

In order to restore the cornerstone of your financial strength, you must start wearing 3-D glasses. You must identify and vigilantly monitor the three core components of financial enslavement: debt, delinquency, and deficit. These three elements often serve as barometers of an individual's or a family's financial health.

The levels of household *debt* threaten our ability to develop any meaningful wealth or to pass that wealth on to future generations. According to the Federal Reserve Board, about one-third of lower-income families spend more than 40 percent of their income on debt repayment, compared to 20 percent for moderate-income households and 14 percent for middle-income families.

Advocacy organization Demos reports, "Credit card debt continues to threaten the financial stability of many low- and middle-income families in the United States, hampering their ability to save and move up the economic ladder." Obviously, the riptide of consumer debt can reinforce one's inability to rise above it. The more your income is consumed by debt, the more you must borrow to pay for essentials such as food, mortgage or rent, utilities, and transportation. Each month digs the hole deeper, making it harder — but not impossible — to climb out of the hole and stand on solid ground.

Another snare, *delinquency*, emerges within this cycle when we cannot pay our bills on time. Late payments lower our credit scores, which in turn can cause us to pay higher interest rates even on strategically reasonable debt, such as mortgages. (Some people call this "good debt" because it is secured by an asset.) Late fees, higher interest rate penalties, and lower credit scores not only increase the amount of our debt but they usually discourage and dishearten our desire to fight. Looking for emotional comfort from our desperate situation, we may be tempted to spend, charge, or borrow even more. If we are serious about our fiscal freedom, we must commit to eliminating such delinquency. Simply put, this commitment honors our pledge to pay all of our bills on time.

Finally, we must get to the heart of the problem and change our attitudes and behavior. To be free of *deficit* living means we live within our means and eliminate the need to close our spending gaps by using high-interest credit cards or, even worse, alternative financial services such as payday loans, pawnshops, and rent-to-own schemes.

These three objectives represent the core of being dfree® and ensure lifelong freedom if pursued concurrently, consistently, and conscientiously.

As I learned when I decided to become free from financial slavery, a plethora of information is available for anyone who wants to learn about money and money management. Financial literacy programs, books, and information abound.

However, what's missing is a practical strategy that we can use to identify the false beliefs, inconsistent values, and harmful habits that have kept us locked in comfortable consumer prisons. Our greatest challenge these days is that we still have not recognized our status as economic slaves. This pervasive debt trap, with its slavery of owing money, spending money, and living above our means, is harder to address than the slavery of the past. Those individuals captured, brutalized, and brought to this country against their will over two centuries ago knew they were slaves. They knew the reality of their situation. Consequently, they could and did struggle against their slavery and pursue their freedom in a variety of ways.

The tragedy today is that we're reluctant to admit we're slaves. But unless we're willing to address the root of the problem, we will never experience the financial freedom that's available to us. The only way a sick person can get well is to first admit to being sick. If you're walking around coughing and sneezing and blowing your nose and insisting, "I'm all right — nothing's wrong with me," then your words are undermined by reality.

The only way a weak person can get strong is to admit to being weak. You'll notice in the Gospels when Jesus would encounter people who were sick or lame, he would often say, "Do you want to get well? What do you really want?" (see John 5:2 – 15). He wasn't being insulting or insensitive; he simply knew that the process must begin with individuals embracing the reality of their situation and wanting to change it.

Instead we bury the depth of our indebtedness with more purchases, another vacation, a new car, another loan. The idea that we would voluntarily become slaves is offensive to all of our sensibilities. But when we continue to spend what we don't have, charge what we don't need, and borrow more than we can repay, then we must call the problem what it is: slavery.

I know this firsthand. I was once enslaved to consumer debt. I couldn't even pay my federal income taxes. Consequently, the IRS garnisheed my wages to cover the back tax payments I owed. Lest you think that I haven't learned what I know the hard way, please allow me to share a little of my own story.

The Cost of a Full Tank

My life with "plastic power" began with my naïve assumption that I should accept any credit card a company was willing to give me. After I received my driver's license, my parents helped me buy a *very* used car for cash so I did not have any car payments to make. But the car had a terrible habit of needing a full tank of gas at least once a week. Even though this only amounted to $5 or $6 at the time (if you can imagine that!), an eighteen-year-old unemployed college student was thrilled to receive a new credit card from the Gulf Oil Corporation.

When that gas card arrived in the mail, I thought I'd died and gone to heaven! I drove straight to the gas station and filled my tank. Prior to getting the card, I'd buy whatever I could afford, even a dollar's worth of gas — yes, one dollar — and drive for at least half a week on it. My new plastic card, however, empowered me to buy a full tank anytime I wanted.

It never occurred to me to consider the interest rate my new empowering card would charge me for all those full tanks. Nor did I consider the reality that my financial status would not change between my purchase and the arrival of the credit card bill. I basically ignored the fact that I would need to pay the bill for the gas I charged. After all, I'd entered the world of adulthood. I was a free man. My new life felt so exhilarating that, in some strange way, even the gas I bought seemed to be free. What a life!

A few weeks later, the first credit card bill from Gulf arrived. I was shocked to see how much gas I'd purchased, and it far exceeded what I could muster for a payment. Much to my relief, Gulf did not ask me to pay the entire amount. "What wonderful people," I said to myself. "They must really understand my circumstances. All they want me to pay is $20, and I can pay the rest next month." So I sent Gulf the $20 just as my bill indicated. Meanwhile, I kept using my card to buy gas for the next month.

When the next statement came, I knew the company must have made a mistake. I had sent them $20 toward my previous bill, but my new balance was higher than I expected. On top of this, the cost of all my newly purchased gas had been added to this new balance. When I called the phone number on my bill to ask them what happened to the money I had sent them, a very polite woman explained the situation. She told me that most of the $20 I had paid went to pay interest and the rest was used to pay down the principal. My first introduction to interest payments left me speechless.

The Breaking Point

The Gulf card began a fifteen-year cycle of credit, interest, and penalty payments that I am often too embarrassed to describe. While I established myself publicly as a civil rights activist, community development leader, and proponent for social justice, privately I remained broke and avoided bill collectors on a regular basis. I was preaching about going to heaven but was heading deeper and deeper into financial hell.

Before the people at Gulf realized that I was not the kind of customer they wanted and canceled my card due to constant late payments, I had gotten two airline cards from TWA, an auto loan, and a Diners Club credit card. I had also bought furniture, which the store so generously allowed me to finance, for my apartment. I didn't realize until later that it would take me eight years of minimum payments to pay off my new $400 sofa!

Although I had a good job, it didn't pay me enough to carry snowballing balances on four credit cards. I had little knowledge and no strategy whatsoever for my finances. I had never taken a course, read a book, or even had a serious conversation about credit or credit cards. We didn't really have lengthy conversations about money in our family; my parents assumed I had assimilated their values and frugality.

I now see the irony in my helping to ameliorate the effects of slavery and segregation in my social work while signing up for a different but equally devastating type of slavery of my own through my carefree lifestyle. But at the time, I saw no contradiction between the way I was living and what I did for a living.

It really wasn't until I decided to get married that I realized my financial life was a mess. I realized that no bank would lend me any money for a mortgage to buy a house; I knew I could not afford a decent car; I was embarrassed because I had no money saved; I had no health insurance, no retirement fund, no emergency fund, no budget, and no strategy to improve my conditions. But I was engaged to be married — and the ages of my fiancée and myself suggested that if we were going to have children, we did not have many years to wait. And with the prospect of children coming up, I knew there soon would be greater financial responsibilities.

Not only was I drowning in consumer debt and owner of nothing in my early thirties, I actually was indignant when bill collectors called my house about money I owed. One could probably have diagnosed me as having a mild form of insanity. I say that because when the bill collectors did catch me on the telephone, I began telling them that they should have a much nicer attitude toward me because it was people like me who made it possible for them to have their jobs. I actually told one caller that if I had paid my bill on time, she would have had no one to call. What would she do then? I was so crazy that I tricked myself into believing my tardy bill payments were acts of kindness for the bill collectors. Never mind that my credit score would take years to repair and improve.

One might assume that this was my lowest point. Unfortunately, it got worse. Just a few months before my wedding, I received a certified letter from the United States Treasury Department — not a good sign. Not only did I have this credit and finance problem, I had decided that since I owed so much income tax that I couldn't pay, I would wait to file a return until I had the money. However, the IRS decided that if they did not take some action, they might never hear from me. So they sent me a letter — return receipt requested — that the mail carrier would not release until I signed my name to verify that I had received it. Since I already knew that I owed the IRS money and the approximate amount, I figured there was no need to open the letter. I just put it with the growing stack of other envelopes containing unopened bills.

The next letter from the IRS arrived right after the IRS had taken money from my meager checking account for the back taxes I owed. I opened the letter. This letter said that my failure to respond to their previous notices left them with no choice but to take drastic measures. Here I was on my way to my wedding day and the government was taking the little money I had. They not only wanted my back taxes, they also charged me penalties for failing to file my tax return and interest on both the taxes and the penalties. I didn't have to die and go to hell; I was there and the heat had just gotten hotter.

Loose Change

I made up my mind that I had to change — and I had to change by the time I got married, only weeks away. Once I made my decision, I discovered an unlimited supply of available information which I had simply never noticed or engaged. For instance, as a dedicated music lover, I always listened to my car radio while driving. With my new objective in mind, I discovered that there's much more on the radio than music, including a daily four-hour radio show that featured financial advice. As part of the show's format, people would call in and describe their situation to the host, giving their age and describing their assets, listing liabilities, and explaining their goals. The show's host would then describe various options for them to consider. Soon I was hooked and arrived at three important conclusions.

The first was that I received so much information, I felt like I had stumbled across an entirely new world. I took notes and wrote down terms the host used that I did not understand. Later, I researched the terms to make sure that the next time he used them, I would know what they meant. I wrote down the names of books the host mentioned and then got the books from the library — at no cost — and read them to increase my knowledge. I could not believe that the same radio I had used solely for entertainment was now like the Underground Railroad, helping me to become a truly free man.

My second discovery while listening to the show was that the host always advised people to pay off as much of their debt as possible. He consistently told people that it made no sense having money in a savings account or a certificate of deposit earning perhaps 5 percent interest and also have a credit card balance and pay 18 percent interest. This made perfect sense to me. But I had never heard anyone talk like this before. And there I was paying high interest rates with no savings at all. One thing became clear: I would never have any money if my charge-and-spend mentality did not change.

The final and perhaps most significant discovery was that, as I listened to the callers, I felt humiliated by my lack of initiative. I heard people my age calling the radio show with questions about investment strategies, retirement options, college funds, tax shelter matters, real estate investing, and other assets they owned. Here I was in my early thirties and all I had to show for my life was a stack of newspaper clippings that described my work as I "fought the good fight." These people were my age and they were making plans and taking control of their financial future.

I had never felt so unaccomplished and incomplete. While passionate about social change, I had done nothing about my own personal financial responsibilities. I had proposed solutions for solving huge social problems but had never balanced my own checkbook. I had fought for justice and equality but could not afford to make a donation to a black college, the NAACP, or any other cause I supported. Fortunately, my shame and humiliation motivated me to take actions that would be life changing. In fact, what I now know is that helping people escape the slavery of debt and deficit living *is* the good fight.

If we are to win this fight, then we must develop a practical strategy that we can use to identify the false beliefs, inconsistent values, and harmful habits that have kept us locked in comfortable consumer prisons. Our greatest challenge these days is that we still have not recognized our status as economic slaves. This pervasive debt trap must be acknowledged as a grave problem with consequences every bit as life threatening as the slavery of our nation's past. But until we're willing to open the unopened bills, make the necessary calls, and face the reality of our confinement, we will never experience freedom from financial slavery.

The choice is yours.

2

Address the Mess

Listing Income and Bills,
Securing All Financial Docs

ONE OF THE GREATEST SIGNS OF DISCONTENT IN OUR SOCIETY today is the proliferation of commercial storage facilities. We buy a house or rent an apartment and we fill our closets with clothes, shoes, and other items. When we have no more room in our bedroom closets, we go to the guest room or the kids' rooms. Then when those closets have no more space, our next stop is the basement.

Then we go to the attic — never mind that it may be a fire hazard. We put stuff in the attic that could not fit in the basement or in upstairs closets. Then — you guessed it — we go to the garage and stack boxes and make piles to the point that our car no longer fits. No wonder we need three-car garages — two bays for parking vehicles and one for storing stuff!

When we completely run out of room and/or our spouse keeps reminding us of what an eyesore we've created in the closets, basement, attic, and garage, then it's time to employ one of my favorite storage strategies: "out of sight, out of mind."

No matter whether they're items that we can no longer identify or haven't touched in over five years, we go out and rent space in a storage facility, paying at least $29.99 every month to store our stuff in a secure, temperature-controlled environment.

So why do we have so much stuff? Basically, because we weren't content with what we had, so we bought more shoes than we could ever wear, more pants than we needed, more dresses than we will ever fit in, and more coats than anyone could wear in the coldest climates. We're accumulators suffering from affluenza. The old-fashioned term is simply *pack rats* — holding on to everything even as we search, shop, and scavenge for more — all because we don't know how to be content with what we have.

Culture Shock

The problem is more than just a matter of storing stuff we don't need or even want. A major component of our slavery is cultural conditioning. If we are to escape the shackles of financial slavery, then we must examine and assess our beliefs about money and our relationship to it. Unfortunately, we are bombarded by thousands of explicit and covert messages about who we are, what we need, and what's most important. Simply put, we're conditioned to never have enough of anything.

In his seminal book *The Tipping Point*, Malcolm Gladwell argues rather effectively that cultures can change — he would call this a social "epidemic" — where ideas spread as a result of "seemingly inconsequential personal influences." In the years since his book was written, I believe we are now in a social "pandemic" of constant marketing, spinning, selling, and incentivizing. We are living in the midst of some of the most shocking changes in our culture that have ever occurred.

Some of these changes emerge as the result of technologies that affect our everyday lives. For instance, there has been a culture change in interpersonal communications. We don't sit down and handwrite and mail letters to our relatives, friends, or acquaintances anymore. We send them emails or texts, drop them a line on Twitter, or post a note on their Facebook wall. Many people don't spend the kind of time cooking meals in the kitchen as they once did — they buy precooked meals to heat in a microwave oven, drive through the fast-food joint down the block, or order takeout from their favorite restaurant.

Other changes emanate not from developments in technology but rather from shifts in our beliefs and our worldviews. Who would have thought fifty years ago that we would hear profanity, see nudity, and witness violence as a regular feature on network television? Because our beliefs have changed as a culture, we now tolerate what we would have found offensive and immoral just a few decades ago. Traditional values and mores have changed so drastically that most of our grandparents either do not recognize or would not want to witness how our culture has evolved from theirs.

If we are to claim our freedom from debt, delinquency, and deficits, then we must rise above the cultural pressures to remain enslaved. We must admit our own problem and open our eyes to all the cultural influences that bombard us with deficient data to feed our self-delusions. Our cultural acceptance of debt has resulted in bad credit, car repossessions, denied credit applications, canceled credit cards, and a desperate marginality in the quality of our lives. To reclaim our freedom we must examine the cultural messages regarding money, connect the dots to our own perceptions and habits, and then chart a course for change. It may be a bit painful, but let's listen to the conversation between our culture and your mind.

You Are What You Buy

In the beginning, we learned that when we're hungry, it feels good to eat until we're full. As we got older, it was also very satisfying to receive a new toy, enjoy a special event, or invite a friend over to play. Later, we learned about satisfying other appetites and achieving other rewards on a larger scale — a career, a spouse, a family, a home. In countless ways, we've learned that it feels good to get what we want. Or what we *think* we want. Over the course of our lifetime, we've learned to be expert *consumers*.

I understand the economic theory that motivates political leaders to say we need more spending to strengthen the economy. But the solution to our problem is not more spending, it is more control over what we spend and not spending what we don't have to purchase what we don't need or even want in many cases. Spending is the defining — and confining — behavior of financial slaves. Basically, three types of spending determine the manner in which we handle our money.

Compensatory spending seeks to compensate for a sense of unworthiness and thereby seeks to gain significance. Simply put, we become consumers who are trying to compensate for our weaknesses, insecurities, and perceived deficits. We try to define ourselves, create an identity, and express our feelings by what we wear and drive, where we work and shop — even where we go to church.

Almost every day of our lives, we get a message from somewhere that tells us, "You really don't matter." And so, subconsciously, we will spend money to gain the feeling of significance that we fail to have in our relationships. We will buy things because, consciously recognized or not, we have these thoughts and feelings: "If my spouse does not affirm me, if my girlfriend does not encourage me, if my teacher does not believe in me, if my family does not support me — then I will find a way to get what I need without them. If my society doesn't seem to recognize me, then I'm going to 'buy me something' and be somebody. I'll show them!" Can you see how it happens?

The Cost of Compensation

A cursory look at advertisements quickly reveals how most retailers try to convince us that we *need* their products to have significance and success. If you purchase this kind of car, then you're sexy *and* smart. Women who wear this brand of perfume are beautiful and wildly exotic. This computer game will allow you to escape to another world. This cleaning product is what good homemakers use to please their families.

Through such constant images, sound tracks, and words, the message becomes an insistent refrain: "If you just buy our product, you'll be such a better everything!" As if our personal significance is enhanced by purchasing and using any particular product! Unfortunately, we buy into the illusion again and again and again. We willingly put ourselves deeper in debt and deeper in slavery by buying new clothes when we already have a closet full of nice clothes, by buying the latest sports car when our five-year-old sedan runs just fine. Why do we work so hard to support something that's simply not true?

Basically, we pay for a consolation prize. We may not be able to control other people and prevent them from disappointing and hurting us. We may not be able to control our work environment or our spouse's temper. But we will control how we look, what we drive, and how others perceive us — no matter how much it costs. The only problem, however, is that nothing we purchase has the power to console us, to compensate for unfulfilled emotions, or to replace the power — and heartache — of human relationships.

If we step back and look at this problem and become honest with ourselves, we soon realize that what we really need, money cannot buy. I love that song Dionne Warwick recorded years ago, "A House Is Not a Home," because of the way it expresses this truth. Money can buy a house, but money can't make a home. Money can buy medicine, but money can't make us healthy. Money can pay for fun, but money can't give us joy.

Money allows us to travel, but it cannot secure our eternal destination. Money allows us to buy as many books as we want, but money can't make us intelligent. Money can buy sex, but money can't buy love. Money can buy busyness, but money can't buy purpose. Money can buy food, but money can't buy the intimacy of breaking bread with another human being.

Think of compensatory spending as our attempt to level the playing field of life. People and events beyond our control pull us down, so we buy things to make us feel better, to replace our loss. But the things we really need in life, money cannot buy.

Fake It 'til You Make It

The second kind of spending goes beyond leveling the playing field. *Conspicuous spending* attempts to elevate your game to a whole new level. According to the late-nineteenth- and early-twentieth-century sociologist and economist Thorstein Veblen, people will spend wastefully in order to become part of what he called the new "leisure class," which was growing alongside the emerging wealth of Vanderbilt, Astor, Carnegie, and others.

Writer and social critic Vance Packard advanced this theme in his 1957 book *Status Seekers* in which he tracks the relationship between consumer spending and perceived social status. He found that to the extent that moving into higher classes became a cultural priority, spending as if we were already there became an equally compelling habit.

Or, as we called it when I was coming up, "Fake it 'til you make it." This type of spending attempts to purchase social status by looking the part, dressing the part, driving the part, and living the part of someone who is already wildly successful and ridiculously wealthy. This mind-set pervades our culture today through the ubiquitous presence of "designer brands." When faced with the choice between two white shirts — identical in fabric and construction — the conspicuous consumer pays $50 more for the one that shouts, from the mouth of a tiny polo player, alligator, eagle, swoosh, stripe, or star, "I'm successful and have good taste — look at me!"

We have been conned and conditioned into believing our social status is achieved by spending money on items that cost more than they should. And we will spend $50, $100, or more for the famous logo because it communicates that we are well-off, stylish, and successful. The logo indicates that we're in the know, hip, cool, up-to-date, fresh, phat, bad, and the best — all because we have enough money to buy the shirt with the logo on it. Such purchases create a certain status, and we can then hang around with other people who wear the same labels.

If our status is sought through external things, it's no wonder we spend money we don't have. We have to keep up with our own status. It's not the Joneses we're striving to keep up with and emulate. Most of us are trying to keep up with ourselves, with our own self-imposed definitions of worth, success, and value. We see images of other people and develop this persona we want to create and cultivate as a substitute for the high-risk vulnerability of being our genuine selves. We want to belong, to be cool, to be special, to be normal, to be accepted, to be admired, to be remembered.

Buying in to this mind game keeps us in financial slavery. We can't make it if all we do is fake it. We think we're in control of our money, but our psychological dependence and emotionally motivated expenditures reveal just the contrary: our money is controlling us.

Not Getting Our Money's Worth

So we have *compensatory spending* for the purpose of gaining significance and *conspicuous spending* for the purpose of elevating and flaunting status. Finally, we have *confused spending*, those purchases which we make without stopping to think, analyze, or assess the cost-benefit of what we're actually getting for our money.

Whether we're uninformed, haven't done our homework

and compared prices for the best value, or just don't care, such behavior leads to poor choices, and soon the poor have fewer and fewer choices to make. In my humble opinion, consumer confusion propels a company like Starbucks to its stellar heights of success. Why would millions of people become so enamored, even addicted, to a cup of coffee that costs $4.50? Are we that devoted to the coffee and its exotic names and flavors? Do we really feel better knowing we're drinking coffee that comes from Guatemala, Ethiopia, or the Sudan? Is what we're getting in our cup of coffee worth what we're paying?

When I was growing up, Chock Full o' Nuts coffee was popular. It was known as the "heavenly coffee." However, even if those beans had been grown in heaven, no one on earth was about to pay $4.50 for a cup of it! It would have been considered ridiculous, if not outright stupid, spending.

It takes a strong commitment to wise spending and an ability to see beyond the present moment to clarify any confusion clouding a potential purchase. You must be willing to delay gratification and walk across the parking lot to the free drinking fountain when you're thirsty instead of buying a bottle of water. You must plan ahead. Anticipate that your kids will be hungry after shopping all morning and bring snacks along instead of automatically succumbing to their pleas for drive-thru fast food.

If you make a commitment to yourself and your freedom never to make an impulse purchase at the checkout line, then do not make exceptions. Some people know their own weaknesses and avoid going in certain stores or shops, just as a recovering alcoholic avoids bars and liquor stores. For others, the solution to overcoming confused consumer habits is simply to come up with a plan, which I'll walk you through in chapter 4, and purchase only what's in the plan. If you have large purchases to make, it's especially wise to do research online, compare brands and customer reviews, and shop around for the best value.

While compensatory and conspicuous spending have psychological and emotional roots, the hold of confused spending is more a matter of convenience, indifference, and ignorance. As you begin to gather together the details of your financial life and track where it all goes, it becomes easier to notice where you're hemorrhaging by nickels and dimes. It may be the daily Starbucks or fast-food lunch. Maybe it's your impulsive nature that doesn't like to slow down. Whatever the case, confused spending may be the easiest to curb and control.

Treasure Hunt

If you're serious about breaking the chains of financial slavery, then you must examine the psychology of your spending habits and explore the emotions attached to money-related matters. If you're validating your worth by creating a mask of material possessions, then you will never be free. If you're expressing yourself and celebrating who you are only through your next purchase, then you'll remain imprisoned.

We must learn to replace the harmful ingredients in the culture of debt with life-giving agents of clarity, freedom, and responsibility.

I am aware that not everyone spends his or her way into debt as I did. Many people lost their jobs and, while unemployed, relied on credit cards and other types of borrowing just to make ends meet. Others had health challenges that caused the bills for doctors, medicine, tests, and even hospital visits to pile up. Still others borrowed money to pay for college, thinking their education would qualify them for jobs that would enable them to repay their loans. And then there are those whose marriage ended in divorce, and they ended up being responsible for the debt their former spouse incurred. The point is that living in debt is too stressful and damaging to accept as a lifestyle. The old spiritual, Oh Freedom, inspires us with its passionate words: "And before I'd be a slave I'd be buried in my grave!"

The beginning of this process is to face the reality of your situation, one step at a time, one day at a time. For many people who deliberately keep their heads in the sand to avoid the painful reality of their financial slavery, it's going to require more courage than education. For others who are enthusiastic about taking control of their financial responsibilities, the process may be more about learning some basics than unraveling motives.

In either case, it never hurts to start with the basics. As you gather all the pieces of information related to your finances, think of it as a treasure hunt. You're now searching for the key to your freedom, the solution to your slavery, and it's right there in between your mortgage payment and the weekly dry-cleaning bill. If you tend to hate focusing on these kinds of details, then it will be critically important to focus on why you're gathering these items in order to attain your ultimate goal of financial freedom. To reinforce their focus, many people I know like to keep a "goal sheet" in a location (or several) where they see the goal every day.

One woman who participated in our dfree® program liked to hang a photograph of a beautiful tropical beach scene above the desk where she paid bills and went over her finances. The serenity of the scene reminded her to stay calm, and the beauty of it inspired her to save for the dream vacation she had always wanted but could never afford. With a tangible reward established for her goal of financial freedom, she remained motivated to face the details on a daily basis.

First, make a list of all sources of monthly income you presently receive: salary, bonuses, pension, consulting fees, commissions, and everything that brings in money on a consistent basis each month. After you've listed everything, add all the amounts to determine your monthly income. Unless you own your own business, this amount should be your net income, not your gross income. People who are self-employed or own a small business need to make sure they use net numbers too, after quarterly state and federal taxes have been paid.

Next, gather all your bills, debts, loans, and anything else you owe to anyone, whether bank, credit union, employer, friend, or relative. While you can compile your list in a variety of ways, I encourage you to list them in the way that makes the most sense to you.

The key is to list all your debts and ongoing expenses. Whether you write them out by hand with pencil and paper, make your own spreadsheet, or use a software template, it doesn't matter as long as it makes sense to you. Don't forget to include cost-of-living expenses such as food, clothing, gifts, eating out, transportation, vehicle maintenance, and home maintenance. As painful as it may be, tally them all.

When I look at my financial obligations, I like to have three amounts for each one: (1) the amount I owe this month; (2) the average of this amount for the prior twelve-month period (this will be the same for many bills, especially those with fixed payments, but will vary with fluctuating expenses such as food, utilities, and transportation); and (3) the balance remaining on what I owe to this creditor. These three figures allow me to see both the immediate amount for this month as well as a context for the big picture of this debt. I like to know the total amount I owe on everything combined.

Now for the side-by-side comparison of income to outgo. How does the total amount of money that comes in to you each month compare to the total amount going out? How much do you have left over? Or, more likely for many of us, how much are we short each month? In either case, what do you do about the difference? Are you saving what's left over or spending it? If you're short on funds each month, how are you covering the difference? By charging groceries? Cash advances on paychecks? Credit card cash advances to make a payment on another bill?

The next step for now is to gather all other documents and data points for your finances. You will need to know the annual percentage rates (APRs) on your credit cards, the percentage rate on your mortgage and car payments, and the dollar amount of late fees they charge. Gather all the puzzle pieces together and organize them all in one place — a large notebook, accordion folder, or document on your computer. Whatever works for you. Here's a list of items you'll want to collect before completing your financial snapshot:

- [ ] Pay stubs for the past month
- [ ] Annual income taxes withheld (W-2s) and property taxes paid
- [ ] Savings and investment account statements
- [ ] Retirement account statements — IRAs, 401(k)s, 403(b)s, pensions, etc.

- [ ] Monthly contribution amounts to your savings/ investment account(s)
- [ ] Insurance premiums for auto, home, health, group plans, and life
- [ ] Insurance policies, benefits, and distributions and/or recent statements
- [ ] Loan statements — home mortgage, installment loans, credit cards, etc.)
- [ ] Company benefits statements
- [ ] General household expense information — food expenses, utilities, maintenance, etc.

Yes, it can be daunting to begin facing the ugly truth about your financial slavery. But remember that each chapter of this book you read, each item on the above list you collect, each day that you change an old habit is a step toward freedom for the rest of your life.

Take a deep breath and be honest with yourself. Do you want to be free? Then it's vital for you to know exactly what it is that's binding you. You must face the objective financial data in order to begin your subjective pursuit of liberty. It's like wanting to lose weight — you must be aware of what you're eating and how much you weigh in order to have a baseline; you must step on the bathroom scale.

Be accurate with your figures. Don't try to soften the edges by rounding down or guesstimating on your debt. It's crucial that you tell yourself the truth about where you are if you're ever going to get where you want to be — free to experience the joy of full financial mobility.

3

Adjust the Attitude

Establishing Life Goals,
Changing Motivation

IN THE 2009 MOVIE *TAKEN*, ACTOR LIAM NEESON PLAYS THE role of a retired Secret Service agent whose teenage daughter wants to travel to Europe with friends. Her mother, divorced from her father, is willing to let the seventeen-year-old take the trip. However, as a minor, the young woman needs her father's permission as well in order to leave the country, and he remains adamant about her not going. The child thinks her dad is being the meanest person in the world. But he's truly only being cautious on her behalf in light of how dangerous he knows Europe can be for an attractive, young, naive female.

After reluctantly giving in to the pressures of his ex-wife and irrational daughter, the father consents to the trip, only to be called within hours of her arrival with the news of her abduction and the murder of her friend. The rest of the movie follows this passionate father's search for his daughter, drawing on all of his strengths and skills as a former agent to rescue her. After the ordeal, the girl and her mother recognize the wisdom of the father's original position and wish they had listened to him. Instead, they experienced life-threatening danger and soul-wrenching anguish before they could understand his perspective.

Similarly, admitting the problem of our financial slavery and sorting through the details of the mess we've made of our finances is not enough to produce change. Our attitude must change if we are to follow through and change behaviors and habits that continue to jeopardize our financial health. The only way to change our attitude in a way that addresses our problem head-on is to realize what we truly long for and the one Source who can provide it.

To Hell and Back

The plot of *Taken* reminds me of another story in which a child demands to leave home only to find himself in dire straits that could have been avoided. We commonly refer to it as the parable of the "prodigal son." In one of Jesus' most famous stories (Luke 15:11 – 32), he describes a timeless family triangle: an industrious father who has done well for himself, an impatient son who makes a fool of himself, and a jealous brother who gets beside himself. The story's catalyst is the demand by an impulsive young man for immediate access to the inheritance he'll receive upon his father's death.

After the young man gets his money, he quickly turns his new prosperity into devastating poverty. It doesn't take long for him to burn through his cash with carousing, drinking, and partying. In short, he makes a total mess of his life. This fellow, who was accustomed to living well in his father's house, ends up losing his inheritance, forced to feed pigs and sleeping on the ground. The great tragedy of his story is that he was entirely responsible for his plight.

He was not poor because he was beaten and robbed like the traveler on the road to Jericho in Jesus' parable of the good Samaritan. He was not poor as a result of being kidnapped from his home and then deserted by his family. He was not living as an oppressed beggar as a result of political circumstances over which he had no control. No, this young man chose his "prodigal" status. His character splinters along the fault line of his own greed, impatience, and entitlement.

He didn't consider the long-term benefits of planning and working for what he wanted. He couldn't wait for his father to die, so he demanded his share up front. Without worrying about the consequences or where his decisions would lead, the young man spent his money on extravagant excess only to find himself bankrupt, financially and emotionally. He went from the stable home life of his father's house to the unbridled debauchery of his spendthrift ways to the bottom of a bucket of pigs' slop. This young man had not died and gone to hell, but his life had become a living hell.

Too many people today live just like this young man — experiencing a hellish existence of their own making. They may not be living outdoors and dwelling with swine, but too many people are living in a spiritual and financial hell. When we live for things we cannot afford — willing to do just about anything to acquire more stuff — we're already in hell. When we spend money we don't have, that we don't know when we are going to get, we're already living in hell. When we go to work every day and cannot write a check without worrying about having sufficient funds to cover it, we're living in hell.

Jesus tells the parable of the prodigal to explain that God

loves us whenever we are ready to be loved. This is the great news that resounds from the story of the prodigal son. But the reality incorporated in the story's plot is that financial irresponsibility is tantamount to sin and likened to death. The father described his son as having been "dead ... lost" (Luke 15:32), because the youth had been living in hell. And he got entangled in hell by his inability to wait for his inheritance and his inability to make good decisions about spending money. Wasting his money was the route he took to a hellish self-imprisonment.

While I recognize that this parable is not primarily about money, it's striking how often, throughout the Gospels, Jesus uses stories that involve money to teach spiritual lessons. It's almost as if Jesus focuses on the familiar commodity of money in order to teach us how to relate to and understand God. From my own experiences and the numerous dfree® participants I've met, I've learned that managing money is a great way to practice and understand our spiritual relationship with God.

The steps we must take to fix our financial problems are the same steps that draw us closer to our ultimate longing, the intimacy of relationship with a heavenly Father who created us, knows us, and loves us. The story of the prodigal son makes this so clear that it's often called, more aptly, the story of the loving father. For when the prodigal does return home, humbled and willing to work as a servant in his father's house, his daddy runs down the road to meet him, gives him a huge bear hug, and then throws a lavish welcome-home party. "I thought my son was dead," the father explains, "but now he's alive and back home with me." The good news is that his son escaped from his self-imposed hell. And the good news is that we can get out of our living hell too.

When the young man was at his lowest, the one thing that happened to get him out of his hell was that he saw himself. He realized he had hit rock bottom. He assessed his situation and knew he was in trouble. This is the first thing we have to do to get out of financial hell — we have to admit that we are in hell and we have to want to get out.

Paying Our Ransom

If we are going to get out of our hell, we have to own the bad choices we've made and the current hole we're in. It's humbling, but so is having a car repossessed or losing a home in a foreclosure. I remember when I was living in hell and basically "sleeping with swine." I was twenty-three and driving a brand-new car that seemed bigger than my rented apartment. My car payments were almost half of my salary. I was paying the previous month's bills with next week's paycheck. I would write checks and hope I could get money in the bank before the check bounced. My favorite response became "I don't know where my money goes," as if it just mysteriously evaporated from my bank account and wallet.

No, I did not want to account for where it went because that would've meant responsibility. That would have meant refraining from some of my frivolous "essential" expenditures. I was a lost son guilty of wasteful extravagance and unable to help anyone or any cause because I was pretty on the outside and penniless on the inside. I had no insurance, no savings, no plan — and no hope of change.

Like the young man in the story, I could not change until

Level I: Started

I saw myself. It is so easy to see others. We not only see others' physical traits, we also recognize the spiritual flaws in others. But Jesus challenges us to see ourselves. He chastised the Pharisees about seeing the speck in others' eyes and missing the planks that were in their own eyes (Luke 6:41–42).

This is the message for us. We can no longer afford to see what is wrong with others and ignore what is wrong with us. We are called upon to see ourselves, and, if we are living in hell, we need to tell the truth about ourselves to ourselves. If you are addicted to shopping, if you are living above your means, if you are wasting and losing money due to an addiction to gambling, tell the truth — tell it to yourself.

This is how the prodigal son got out of his hell. After he honestly saw himself, then he spoke to himself. There comes a time in life when we have to talk to ourselves. There comes a time in life when the minister cannot talk to us, the counselor or therapist cannot talk to us, our parents or spouses cannot talk to us — we must address ourselves. When you talk to yourself, make sure no one is listening so that you can really tell the truth. When the prodigal son talked to himself, he said, "How many of my father's hired men have food to spare, and here I am starving to death!" (Luke 15:17). These were words only he could say to himself.

This is how we get better spiritually and make a permanent adjustment in our attitude. There comes a time when our parents cannot beg us to go to church. There comes a time when our grandparents can't keep nagging us about doing something with our lives. There comes a time when we must talk to ourselves. This is how we get right with God — we start by talking to ourselves.

This is also how you get out of debt and financial hell —

you must have a one-on-one talk with yourself. One way to begin this conversation with yourself is to compile a written list of everything you buy, everything you spend money on. Write down the cost of every newspaper, magazine, cup of coffee, and breath mint. Think through what you spend and why you spend it in an average week — write down the full amount you spend for groceries and eating in restaurants, parking or taking the subway, fast food, and dry cleaning.

With this kind of written evidence of your conversation, you will have answered the question: "Where does my money go?" You will see exactly where and how you are spending your money. Within a month you will be able to account for all your expenses and tell yourself what you need to change.

This practice of writing down an inventory of expenditures could apply equally well to your spiritual life. Becoming more aware of our thoughts and how they translate into attitudes and get actualized in our behavior can benefit every area of our lives.

Our real challenge has less to do with controlling our money and more to do with personal discipline and controlling our lives. Our money is out of control because our lives are out of control. Talk to yourself and say, "Self, it is time for us to get together and stop letting cars and food and clothing come between us."

The prodigal son talked to himself and ultimately got out of hell. But then he submitted himself to his father. He realized that he had to go back to his father's house. Daddy's house was not just an address and a square meal. Daddy's house was a system. In his father's house he knew he would have substance and structure. In his father's house he would have rules and responsibility. In his father's house he would have to submit to his father's approach to life. But he wanted out of hell, and submission was a small price to pay as an alternative to living with swine.

To get out of our financial hell, we have to do what the prodigal son did and submit to a new system that can save us from ourselves. When I found myself living in financial hell, I had to submit to a new system, a new approach to living. Giving the first 10 percent of our income to God — which Christians call "tithing" — is better understood as a key part of God's system. Saving and investing the next 20 percent of our income — this too is part of this new financial system. Balancing our checkbooks and living within a budget — these are all part of the system. Gone is the reckless extravagance of buying what one does not need, spending what one does not have, and living with no financial system in place.

But changing our attitude and accompanying behavior can be easier said than done. I remember once taking my car to the car dealer where I bought the car to get my brakes fixed. I was angry because the car was not very old and my brakes should have lasted longer than they did. I assumed that my brakes must have been defective. So I asked the dealer to change my brakes at no charge. He was not willing to comply with my request. When I challenged him, he told me that my problem was not the brakes on the car; my problem was the way I was driving. Until I changed the way I drove, my brakes would always have problems.

Too many of us treat our problems the way I treated my brakes. We want God to fix our problems without any effort on our part. But God wants us to change the way we live. God wants us to change our system because God wants to change our hearts.

Trying harder to be a good, moral person is not the answer.

Attending church is not the solution. Studying the Bible more often is not the solution. These are all worthwhile endeavors, but unless you're pursuing them out of your longing to know God, to love God, and to serve God, they won't change you. Only a relationship with the Savior can change us.

Jesus died to change the system. He died to change the way we deal with our enemies. He died to change the way we treat our neighbors. He died to change the way we treat our children. He died to change the way we treat our families. He died to change the way we treat ourselves. He died to change the way we treat our finances.

Turning away from ourselves, from our own extravagant pig troughs, and turning toward Jesus leads us out of slavery, out of hell. He came to set the captives free and heal us of more than our physical ailments. He came to deliver us from the hell we often create for ourselves.

Sampling Jesus

Spiritual transformation involves more than studying Jesus. Having our lives transformed involves counting the cost of pursuing our heart's true desire; it involves following the example that Christ set for us. The apostle Paul invited Christians to follow his example as he was following the example of Christ (1 Corinthians 11:1). It is logical to conclude that Paul was actually inviting us to follow the example of Christ. With all the struggles that Paul reported in his letter to the Romans, I can't believe that he would ask anyone to follow his example. His point was that we should see, follow, and imitate Jesus.

When we were young basketball players, people who knew

us and followed basketball could tell which professional players we admired because we imitated their game in the way we played our game.

Young hip-hop producers practice something that they call "sampling" when they produce their music. They write their own lyrics and then they borrow or "sample" music from "back in the day" — usually R&B music that was so good, there is neither any need nor any way they could ever produce music so great. What is so humorous about this is that many young people today learn the music of yesterday by listening to hip-hop music, and they never realize they are listening to my generation's music. They think the hip-hop guys and gals have created new stuff when, in fact, all they did was "sample" old stuff.

This is what Christians actually do with Jesus. We don't really have to create original ideas about love or justice or faith or finances. All we have to do is "sample" Jesus, and our discipleship grows. When people ask me about my ideas and how I come up with them, I simply remind them that Jesus wrote the script; I just put it to different background music. The dfree® program is really just an example of us "sampling" Jesus. We have placed Jesus' teaching about finance in our packaging for today's environment.

It is one thing to teach about better money management; it something much more profound to experience it as part of our spiritual life transformation. It is good to teach people to live with a budget; it is even better when a Christian knows that he or she is doing that to be like Jesus. Asking people to separate themselves and their identities from their possessions is valid; but showing them that Jesus requires that Christians deny themselves is even stronger.

3. Adjust the Attitude

Unfortunately, our culture is saturated with messages that promote the materialism that produces insecurity and anxiety. These cultural messages reinforce our financial slavery. That's why our attitude shift is critical. To counter this assault by so many forces around us, in the dfree® program we sum up our commitment to debt-free living with a pledge that summarizes our core principles. The words hold no magic power or serve as any kind of supernatural spell. They simply remind us of what it takes to be free.

I *pledge to:*

Apply God's strategy for managing my money

Keep my expenses below my income

Pay my bills on time

Invest in assets that grow in value

Contribute to my church and its ministries

Fortunately, as we follow the example of Christ and pursue our relationship with our Father, we can break the bondage of this lust for things and the anxiety that accompanies it. As Christians, we must replace our preoccupation with the material with the Messiah and redirect our pursuit of stuff with the pursuit of the Savior. When we put our minds to it, set our actions in motion, and invest our complete faith in God, we can do more than resist the power of culture over us. We can experience the freedom and fulfillment that's truly priceless.

Get
CONTROL

"I am a 48-year-old single mother, with an annual income of $52K. My accumulated debt resulted from not receiving child support and having to pay rent, day care expenses, car note, food, clothes, and other day-to-day expenses. When I was able to buy my home, it required maintenance so I took out a second mortgage. My current relationship recently fell apart and all that we spent and planned on paying together is now mine to resolve.

"When I first contacted people involved with dfree®, I was at the point where I could not sleep nor eat. My thoughts were on which creditor would be calling me tomorrow and how I would keep my promises to pay.

"Since I took that first class, I learned what I was doing wrong. I was paying on the creditors' schedule and not mine. I was paying their amounts and not what was suitable for me to maintain my household. I then contacted them with more authority in my way of speaking and with knowledge of my debts and income. Instead of speaking with the representative who answered, I requested to speak with someone with authority to make changes.

"Regarding my home, I attempted to modify my first mortgage but was told because I am not behind and have an FHA loan that I did not qualify. Regarding my credit cards, I was able to change my payment due dates to meet my schedule. I then obtained a second job, working five evenings a week not far from my primary job. This is nice since I'm burning the same amount of gas traveling to and from work.

"My credit card debt has now decreased from $35K to $28K, and my total debt including my second mortgage is below $100K. Although I am not in the clear, I have the confidence that I will be emancipated from the slavery to debt. Thank you for developing this program and having the vision so long ago to provide a solution for the problem that today enslaves so many of us."

Anita C., Short Hills, New Jersey

4

Start the Plan

Creating a Spending Plan, Becoming Accountable

I USED TO ENJOY WATCHING *THIS OLD HOUSE* ON PUBLIC TELE-
vision (PBS) and seeing the transformation of a run-down,
dilapidated home into a beautiful showplace. The construction crew and carpenters made it look so easy and methodical,
replacing worn-out beams with new wood or updating features
with the convenience of technology. More recently, I've seen
the program *Extreme Home Makeover*, sort of the same prem-
ise on steroids. That crew comes in to a family financially
and emotionally desperate and transforms their inadequate,
ramshackle abode into a mansion befitting a spread in *Better
Homes and Gardens* — in only a week!

My own experiences, however, particularly with the
church building campaign that I mentioned earlier, tell me
that the process of renovation is an arduous undertaking. For
our church, what started in 1937 as an abandoned gas station
being rented by a handful of people for $4 a week resulted in
an 80,000-square-foot worship center being constructed on an

adjacent site in 2003. The new facility's auxiliary chapel alone is almost as large as the main sanctuary in the old church. Obviously, this transformation did not happen in a week; it took decades. Even after we had broken ground on the new building site, it was still several years before the structure materialized.

Renovating and rebuilding your financial house takes time as well. You did not arrive at your current level of debt overnight. A financial renovation requires a sound blueprint for rebuilding the structure of your relationship with money. You must develop a spending plan that will serve as your guide in knowing where to rebuild, who to enlist for help, and how long it's going to take to complete.

Count the Cost

If our financial house is infested with parasitic debt and about to collapse in upon itself, then we must remove the rotted wood and start building a house that can withstand our weaknesses. As we've seen earlier, when we come to our senses concerning our financial slavery, then we must leave the pig troughs and return to the waiting arms of our Father. We must address the inner motivation that compelled us to wander in the first place and then reestablish our true focus.

Jesus provides us with clear instruction on how to begin formulating a strategy for debt-free living. While this may not be His primary focus, He's clearly concerned with the whole person, and this includes our burdens, our idols, the forces that enslave us. As Christians, we can always depend on Jesus to tell us what we need. One of his primary teaching tools is the use of parables.

4. Start the Plan

Beginning with Luke 14:28, Jesus shares a series of related parables that focus on the essence of spiritual change, a process that we describe as "sanctification and discipleship." Fundamentally, Jesus is providing oblique answers to the central questions that He received from His followers then and continues to receive today: What exactly does it take to really be your follower? What does it mean to be a Christian, and what's it going to cost me? What will I get in return for what it costs?

He begins, quite literally, with the foundation. Verse 28 says, "Suppose one of you wants to build a tower." You can replace the word *tower* with *house*. Suppose one of you wants to build a house; or, suppose one of you wants to send your child to college; or suppose one of you wants to buy a suit or start a business or lead a church. In other words, Jesus uses this "tower" simply as a symbol of anything that requires something from us, anything that costs us money. "Suppose one of you wants to build a tower," Jesus begins. "Will he not first sit down and estimate the cost …?" The New King James Version says "count the cost." What we normally call "counting the cost" is "preparing a spending plan or a budget."

If you're going to build a house, if you're going to buy a tie, if you're going to go on a trip, why don't you first prepare a budget or a spending plan? "First sit down and estimate the cost to see if he [or she] has enough money to complete it?" This is Jesus talking and He's talking to people whose question is, "What should I do if I'm trying to be a good disciple?"

Unfortunately, too much religion puts emphasis on "religious magic" and gimmicks, the intangible. This stuff is real. Being a Christian has to involve more than singing nice songs, saying nice slogans, praying nice prayers, and building nice buildings. Being a Christian is a lifestyle. And you can't get any more practical than this. Jesus says, in effect, "If you're My disciple, there shouldn't be anything so weird about you that exempts you from the need to have a budget."

Luke 14:29 says, "For if he lays the foundation and is not able to finish it ..." In other words, if you start building without a budget, if you start spending without a plan, if you live with no sense of direction as it relates to finance and you're not able to finish what you've started, your car will get repossessed, you will have to file bankruptcy, or you may go into foreclosure. If you can't finish what you started, "everyone who sees it will ridicule [laugh at you], saying, 'This fellow began to build and was not able to finish.'" Without a plan, a budget, it's likely we will not be able to pay for the building on which we have already started construction.

How Firm a Foundation

Obviously, this reflection is not who we are as sons and daughters of the King, nor is it an accurate picture of the God we serve. If we are to build or rebuild a strong, storm-proof structure, we will have to be honest about what's needed in "this old house." To break free from the slavery of debt, to get out of this condition, we must admit that enslavement to debt is a real problem.

Next, as we've established, it demands a change of attitude. If your attitude is truly going to change in a way that ignites lasting change, then you must start by laying a firm foundation for your new life of freedom. Fundamentally, any plan that is going to work in advancing your freedom must be fueled by the power of your motivation. Attitude and action go hand in hand. This marriage of motivation and method can be easier to talk about than to actualize, as anyone who has tried to diet can attest.

At our church, we've drawn on the strategy of an organization called Debtors Anonymous. In his book *How to Get Out of Debt, Stay Out of Debt, and Live Prosperously*, which I highly recommend, Jerrold Mundis appropriates the 12-step program of Alcoholics Anonymous for people who realize that they're slaves to debt. It takes the same basic twelve steps, starting with the fact that "I can't handle this myself" and moving to the fact that "I need a Higher Power." In other words, "I need God to help me with this."

One of the key statements in Mundis's book impacts our attitude: "You are not your bank balance." See, this is a major attitude shift. It's a significant mental readjustment that recognizes that I am separate from what I have and what I own because once I can separate my identity from the things I have, when my bank account gets low or when my possessions get old or when I can't keep up with the proverbial Joneses, then I still feel good about myself because I am *me* in spite of what I have. This is the power of shifting your attitude and having it in turn empower new behaviors. If I can only afford a used car with two doors, then I will buy a used car with two doors even though a new car with four doors makes me look more successful. I will not buy something just because I feel I deserve it, because now I know I can't afford it. There is an attitude shift, and my new attitude is that if I can't finish it, I won't start it.

This attitude of incompletion and accepting incompletion has spilled over to every aspect of our lives. "I'll start spending even if I can't finish purchasing that item." "I will start school even though I plan to drop out of school." "I will start a marriage knowing I can get out of it easily."

See, we have a very short-term concept of commitment. "I'll join the church, and if somebody makes me mad, I'll leave next week." In the old days, the old saints stayed in church, no matter what happened. The preacher could be a complete fool and Sister Jones would say, "I ain't leaving my church. Nobody is going to run me out of my church." But now folks will leave the church if they can't get a parking space.

And so there is an attitude shift under way. This is what the old spiritual said: "Before I'd be a slave, I'll be buried in my grave." See, that's an attitude. There is another attitude that says, "I'm just glad to be here. I'll take the crumbs. I'm just glad to be around." Now there's also an attitude that says, "I refuse to be alive and dead at the same time." It's an attitude.

Every attitude shift really comes on the heels of admitting the problem. If I have mail I know contains bills and it's three months old and I refuse to open it because I know what is inside and there is no need to open up a letter asking me for money I don't have, I have a problem. If I'm using a credit card to pay off a credit card even though they've said I'll pay no interest for now, I have a problem. If I find myself shopping and waiting until my wife is not home to sneak what I bought into the house — because I don't want her to know I'm spending money and because if she finds out, she's going to go spend some more money — then we have a problem. If I'm paying off last month's bills with next month's check — if I've spent the money before I make it, I have a problem. If I don't mind paying late fees and say, "Well, I'll just have to pay the fee," I have a problem. And once I realize I have a problem, I need an attitude shift.

4. Start the Plan

After you acknowledge the problem and take responsibility for your own economic freedom by adjusting the attitudes hindering your success, then it's time to take action. You are ready to implement the new habits that will liberate you from financial hell. The first step in your action plan is to select a target date for completing and implementing your new spending plan and prepare for that date. You should have a clear awareness of your financial details and have all necessary information available.

At a basic level, your plan for financial freedom should include three main ingredients: you need to establish the particular goals that will achieve your freedom, decide to whom you will be responsible for reporting your goals' implementation and achievement, and set a time line. As with any new program, it's important at the beginning of the dfree® process to define success by setting measurable goals across regular time intervals and establish ongoing accountability.

Blueprint for Freedom

Successful strategies do not just happen by coincidence or accident. Certain dynamics must exist to enhance the likelihood for success. The dfree® strategy includes three key areas as part of an effective blueprint for success. Foremost, you must clearly identify your central goal. Do you want to pay off all credit card debt? Save 15 percent of your monthly income to purchase a car? Pay bills on time and improve your credit rating?

You must be as specific as possible in identifying and articulating the particular goals that will form the pillars of your plan. Having a goal without a system for reaching that goal is like having a destination without a vehicle. Many systems for debt-free living and financial freedom have been created, and you should investigate as many as possible to see which ones address your situation and are compatible with your ethical and spiritual values.

The second key to a successful plan is assembling the support needed to execute your plan. Great athletes have trainers and coaches; great leaders have mentors and advisers; great businesspeople have dedicated teams and administrative support. Your goals to financial freedom are more likely to be achieved when you're sharing the journey with peers and others who understand where you're coming from and, better yet, where you're going. It is easier to accomplish great things when we are not trying to do them alone.

The flip side of accountability is having a community with whom you can share your milestones; success is not fully achieved until it is recognized and celebrated. And the celebration of success motivates us toward more success. The dfree® strategy builds success into the process so that small victories are achieved and then celebrated. Support groups, like the ones we formed at our church, should be positioned to create affirmation through celebration on a continual basis.

Finally, you must align your plan's implementation with a schedule. While there are a variety of ways to attack your debt, a basic way is simply to create a pay-off calendar. You make a list of all money you owe — mortgage, credit cards, car payments, school loans, everything — and then the amount you owe for each, the amount of the monthly payments, and the length of time at this rate of payment to fulfill your debt. It can be daunting.

The Gallup organization reports that two thirds of people

in this country are living without a spending plan or a budget; among African Americans and Hispanics, the numbers are predictably the highest. Research throughout the past decade consistently reveals that roughly 70 percent of Americans live paycheck to paycheck, with the majority of these people using high-interest loans or credit cards to cover unexpected expenses and emergencies. Without a spending plan, a budget that works, a personal finance spreadsheet — whatever you want to call it — you will never achieve your freedom. If your debt is the elephant in the room that you're trying to eat, then a sound spending plan is your knife and fork.

While there are a variety of ways to arrange the details and do the math, bottom line, your strategy must provide answers for the following questions:

1. What's my income-to-debt ratio? How can I focus on paying off my current debts without incurring more?

2. What emotional and psychological triggers contribute to my current financial slavery?

3. How will I handle these triggers moving forward? What do I need to do differently in order to change my spending habits?

4. Who's going to help me? Who will support and encourage me on this journey to freedom?

5. How long will it take to become financially free? What's going to motivate me to keep going when I'm discouraged and tempted to give up?

The essence of dfree® is to help you experience success in life. We have learned that how we handle money is a reflection of how we handle life. People who mismanage their finances are people who mismanage their lives, because money is just a small part of life. In that sense we really do not manage money at all. We manage life and use money to support our needs and goals. This is a battle. It is very difficult work. The truth is that if people could remedy their financial affairs without assistance, then they would be doing it.

While many people already have the right information in their possession, they've struggled to implement it into their lifestyle. Like diets and other personal pursuits for self-improvement, it's easy to start a new program — and many people begin with enthusiasm and good intentions. Just consider how crowded the gyms and workout facilities are every January and then how attendance has dropped off six weeks later.

Similarly, with programs to improve financial health, many people often begin, but the changes don't stick and fail to have any lasting impact. People start reading books and never finish; they start forming budgets but don't adhere to them; they set aside money in a savings account and spend it the following month. A sale on that new sofa they've had their eye on becomes justification to raid the emergency fund.

No, the difficulty we are confronting is not informational. The problem is emotional, psychological, and spiritual. We need solutions that attack these elements of our problem.

A written spending plan accompanied by a thoughtful strategy that identifies your past weaknesses and provides alternate behaviors can become your map to freedom. Numerous sources provide excellent work sheets and software programs for tracking your spending and designing the blueprint for your spending plan. Here is a basic monthly budget template that you may find helpful in creating target goals for a balanced strategy. I've compiled the percentages from a variety of financial sources as well as the experiences of participants in our dfree® movement.

Tithing/Giving	10%
Savings	10%
Investing/Retirement	5–10%
Emergency Fund	1–2%
Housing	25–35%
Utilities	5–10%
Food	5–10%
Transportation	10–15%
Clothing	5%
Medical/Health/Insurance	5–10%
Personal Discretion	5%
Eating Out and Leisure Activities	5–10%
Debts	5–10%

Keep in mind that this is an ideal budget, a target to move toward. Obviously, as you get started, you will likely have to contribute more than 5 percent toward paying off your debts and cut in other areas, such as eating out, leisure activities, personal discretion, and clothing.

We are accountable to God for outcomes. Jesus' parable about the talents in Matthew 25:14–30 suggests that God is concerned about measurable outcomes. My staff knows my definition of accountability — it is the ability to count! At some point, numbers matter. And if we're serious about our freedom, then we must set some goals that include numbers and new behaviors and commit both to God. Then we can devise strategies that help us reach those specific goals and be accountable to God for executing the strategy and attaining our freedom.

5

Steer the Power

*Making Power Payments,
Starting Power Savings*

WHEN I WAS GROWING UP, MY MOTHER WAS THE QUEEN OF THE store layaway. Mother would find a pair of shoes or a dress at the store that she really wanted to purchase but wouldn't have the money to pay for it at that time. So she would give the store a deposit — maybe $10 or $20 — and the store would hold the item. They would "lay it away" until my mother was able to pay for the item. Then over several weeks or months, Mother would visit the store and add a little more money to continue her payments on the selected item. When she was able to pay off the remaining balance in full, she would proudly bring her new purchase home from the store.

When I recently asked some young people in my church what layaway meant, they had no idea. The concept seemed archaic to them, as outdated as rotary phones and eight-track tapes. We no longer have a culture of delayed gratification where we are willing to wait for an item we want until we can pay for it.

We have become a plastic society that has reversed the process. We used to make payments for a purchase before we obtained it. Now we obtain the item and then we make the payments over time. In my mother's era, there were no interest charges with layaway; now when we "charge it," we pay high interest rates that radically diminish our buying power over the long run.

This inability to wait has not only afflicted our finances it has also permeated our entire existence. We can't invest time into preparing and cooking meals, so we want fast food. Our impatience at traffic signals leads to road rage. We cannot even wait to discover the gender of our children; we want to know now so we can purchase crib, clothes, booties, and blankets in the right color and appropriate style.

We are addicted to fast and cannot tolerate any type of delay — especially with items that we believe will make us happy or contented. And since so much of our happiness comes from what we possess, we can't wait to possess more and more. Why wait until we can afford them when we can have them right now? Many people will pay 29 percent interest on a purchase that they will have depleted, discarded, or destroyed before it's paid for. We want what we want and we want it *now*.

Delay to Get Ahead

With the recent recession as catalyst, layaway has made a comeback at many large retailers, including stores like Kmart and Kohl's. The aspect of layaway that I appreciate most is the willingness to wait patiently before taking possession. As we've seen, in order to reclaim power over our finances, we must adjust our attitude and make a plan. A key part of the dfree® approach to our spending plan is to make power payments and set aside power savings. The secret to regaining our power is to sacrifice what we don't need now in order to gain what we must have later. We must delay immediate gratification if we want to accelerate our emancipation.

One of the best ways to reinforce the delay of immediate gratification that comes with swiping our credit card for a purchase is to own and exercise the power you have to free yourself from financial slavery. In order to get off to a good start in your new pursuit of dfree® living, you must move from losing the power that charging takes from you to taking charge of the power. Many people who find themselves enslaved to debt often feel helpless against the crushing waves of monthly bills, late fees, and unexpected expenses. It's tempting to feel powerless and resign oneself to a desperate cycle of treading water, growing wearier with each month that the waters of debt rise around you.

Dealing with our feelings of powerlessness and victimhood is essential if we are to adjust our attitude and establish new behaviors. Especially regarding finances, most of us can identify some way in which we are victims of someone else's actions — our parents, our spouse, our children, our friends.

In addition, there's no limit to the number of schemes that are designed to take advantage of and exploit those people already enslaved to debt. So many homeowners who signed nothing-down mortgage notes were either poorly represented or fraudulently represented. Many companies that purported to help struggling homeowners were actually criminal enterprises. Most of the debt consolidation companies are not necessarily helping people. They're rolling all of a client's individual payments into one lump sum, renegotiating payments with creditors, and often charging fees for settling debts that were never paid on behalf of the clients. This practice was so widespread that it has been made illegal by recent federal legislation.

It's essential to understand what we sign. Secure professional advice and ask questions when we don't know what we are doing. We cannot be too careful about protecting ourselves, our families, and our assets from those less scrupulous than ourselves.

But the reason we're enslaved to debt is ultimately not something we can blame on a mortgage scam or payday loan rip-off. Most of our problems are self-imposed, the result of our own decisions, and we must learn to take responsibility for what we've done to ourselves. In our reality-TV-show world, victimhood removes all personal responsibility and assigns blame for all of our problems on external sources. Pseudo-therapy experts and pop culture counselors often encourage us to blame our parents, our spouse, our boss, our pastor, our mother-in-law — anyone but ourselves. But the reality we must embrace is that we got ourselves into financial slavery, and we — with God's help — are the only ones who can get us out.

If we do not open our mail and respond to letters that we get from lenders when they repossess our cars or foreclose our homes, we are at fault. If we misrepresent the truth on applications and face consequences for that, we are responsible. If we spend money on things we do not need and then are unable to handle our regular responsibilities, we are responsible. We are victims of nothing except our own pride, vanity, and fear.

Feel the Power

In order to fuel your dfree®-powered plan, you'll want to address three areas: (1) paying the price to sacrifice, (2) paying the price to catch up, and (3) paying the price to get ahead. Let's consider each of these one at a time. First, you must determine the areas where you know you will be changing your spending habits. This tactic goes hand in hand with the foundation of adjusting your attitude and planning a course of action.

And the challenging reality is that changing old habits will be painful at times. You will have to make sacrifices and give up items and experiences that may have been considered inviolate and set in stone in your old thinking. Maybe it's that morning cup of Starbucks coffee on the way to work most weekdays. Maybe it's taking your lunch from home instead of eating in the company cafeteria or the mall food court. Maybe it's going on a "shopping fast" from buying new clothes and shoes for the next few months. Perhaps it's giving up your favorite magazine or newspaper and finding a free, alternative source of news and entertainment online.

For me, it was my neckties! When we started dfree® at our church, I had to commit to something personal and concrete to demonstrate a new level of devotion. I didn't want to come across as someone who had all the answers and had always lived an unblemished, debt-free life. I wanted to emphasize that sacrificing for our financial freedom is an ongoing process. Everyone in the church knew about my fondness for nice neckties — beautiful, handmade, silk ties in a variety of patterns and stripes. After analyzing my life and considering my own spending habits, I realized that I continually bought too many ties, owned too many ties, and gave too much attention to ties. So my new dfree® commitment, in addition to the foundational ones already integrated into my lifestyle, was to stop buying neckties! I was able to make that confession, promise public accountability, and challenge people to follow my lead.

Another consideration for how to refocus your finances is selling some assets. This might mean trading in the German luxury sedan for an American-made midsize. It might mean selling the boat that you cling to but only use two or three times a summer, not to mention the price of docking it and storing it all year. It could be examining your jewelry box and rethinking some of those emotionally charged consolation purchases and selling them on eBay or other online sites. I'm not saying you should sell your engagement ring or your great-grandma's pearl necklace; however, you might consider letting go of those sapphire earrings you bought yourself after realizing you'd gained ten pounds over the summer. If you sell some assets, take the money and apply it to your debt.

You're going to have to do some things differently, and giving up certain habits and changing particular preferences may feel like huge sacrifices at first. The key is to remember what you will be ultimately acquiring — financial freedom, peace of mind, and less stress — for what you're letting go of now.

Line of Attack

Next, in order to make power payments on your debt, you'll need to prioritize your debts and establish a strategy for your line of attack. If you're behind on payments and paying late fees and facing other subsequent penalties (higher APRs, etc.), then these must take urgent precedence over any other payments. Like a millstone around your neck as you attempt to swim across the river, late payments will quickly turn a growing snowball into an avalanche of higher balances and stiffer fees.

If you're current with your payments, I commend you — no small feat in this economy. Nonetheless, you'll need to decide how you want to go about taking bites out of the elephant. There are a variety of ways to approach this prioritization. Many experts recommend that you attack your smallest amounts of debt first so that you can experience the exhilaration of entirely paying off a creditor and bringing that balance to zero. This tactic executed successfully also means that you'll have one less payment on your list of bills each month.

If this method appeals to you, then I recommend making a list of all your debt accounts arranged from smallest to greatest. If some of the smaller balances are within reach to pay off immediately, then do so at once, but only after you have carefully considered the amount you need to cover your entire month's budget. Do not become so overzealous in your enthusiasm to be free that you end up hurting yourself in a few months. Take the long view and accept that it's a day-by-day lifestyle adjustment that you're experiencing.

Another way to prioritize your power payments is to look at the accounts that are escalating the fastest because they have the highest interest rates. By working to pay off account balances on these high-interest-rate debts, you're saving money in the long run. Instead of allowing your living room furniture to cost you literally ten times what it's worth because you took the first-year-same-as-cash-no-interest special and stretched the payments over five years, you pay for it as soon as possible.

In addition, you also change the way you make such purchases by committing to only buying furniture if you have the money to pay for it before that first year after purchase ends. Research shows that most furniture and appliance stores make more money on the credit balances and finance charges of their customers than they do on actual merchandise. This is why they continue to defer payments; they have a long-term view of their business and know they can depend on short-sighted consumers who want immediate gratification.

Better yet, make a commitment as part of your power-payment strategy to use only cash or debit cards for purchases. If you're accustomed to using credit cards for everything — and our culture encourages us — then this may be a gradual process. And you'll need to think through the many reasons — or excuses, I believe — for why people continue to use credit cards even after they're focused on their financial freedom. Things like convenience (debit cards are just as convenient), reward points (what have you used reward points for in the past year?), and priority status when you travel (when did you most recently get ushered into first class on a flight or get upgraded at your hotel because of the particular credit card you used?). Cut through the excuses and find a way to afford whatever you buy and pay for it at the time of purchase.

Regardless of how you prioritize your debt payments, the key is to realize what you are actually purchasing: an unencumbered future of financial freedom. Yes, it can be frustrating to know that you're still paying for short-term expendables like eating out, new clothes, and Christmas decorations from three years ago. At some level, you must let go of whatever regret, guilt, shame, anger, or resentment you may harbor at yourself or others. In its place, you must embrace the priceless feeling of freedom that each payment brings you one step closer to achieving.

The Future Is Now

The third and final component of launching your dfree® power plan is learning to save money and defer gratification — like my mother at the layaway counter — until you can afford to purchase an item that's truly justified. Your savings component should have three tiers: (1) an emergency fund of at least $3,000 that you don't touch except for true emergencies; (2) an ongoing savings or investment account that allows you to accumulate a snowballing nest egg; and (3) a savings account or multiple envelope system for designated annual expenses such as real estate taxes, car maintenance, school tuition, or home upkeep.

The first tier, your emergency fund, should be a non-negotiable in your spending plan and overall financial strategy. Nearly every financial expert agrees that having a cash emergency fund on hand is a vital part of overcoming a reliance on credit and dependence on debt. For many people, simply having an emergency fund with at least $3,000 on hand provides them with a sense of power and control that they haven't experienced when it comes time to pay the bills. It's like a child's security blanket — something to hold on to as a reminder that you can handle whatever comes up. An emergency fund automatically reduces a large portion of your anxiety in worrying over the unexpected curveballs that life throws at all of us.

What happens when the car breaks down and needs new tires? What if the refrigerator quits again and it's time to buy a new one? What if the kids get sick and need to go to the doctor? You can sleep at night without worrying about these and dozens of other scenarios because you know your emergency fund provides you with the necessary resources to handle a crisis. It gives you a financial cushion that prevents you from charging those new tires, the new refrigerator, or the trip to the doctor. So an emergency fund is a necessity; it provides peace of mind and prevents further enslavement to old debt-reliant habits.

Next, a general savings or investment account must become a pillar of your financial future. Even if it's initially only a few dollars each month, just the act of saving some of your money — your money, not the bank's or Macy's or American Express's money that passes through your hands — can be empowering. We'll talk more about long-term investments and retirement planning in level 3, Get Ahead, but setting aside at least 5 percent of your take-home pay if possible each month establishes both the habit and the seed money for accumulating wealth. Eventually, you want your money to work for you instead of holding you captive as its indentured slave. Saving for the future without designating the money for any specific item other than your retirement or future well-being will help you maintain your freedom after you've achieved it.

Finally, you need to establish some kind of savings account or savings system (many experts and past dfree® participants use envelopes and like the concreteness of using cash) for those expenses that do not happen every month but nonetheless must be paid every year. You may pay real estate taxes or school tuition only twice a year. You may have the house power washed and repainted every three years. Your car's regular oil change, tire rotation, and maintenance check may occur every three months. Nevertheless, you must plan accordingly and budget these expenses in your plan each month. This way they will not capsize your spending plan when they do arise on the calendar; you will have planned ahead and you will have the money waiting to cover them.

We can summarize the recipe for our dfree® rocket fuel like this:

The Price of Sacrifice — Power Changes

- Choose the areas where you will cut back in order to pay off your debts faster.

- Sell any assets that you can in order to pay off debts faster.

- Remember why you're doing what you're doing: sacrifice what you don't need now for what you must have later.

The Price of Catching Up — Power Payments

- Prioritize your debts: late payments first.

- Prioritize by choosing to attack the debts with the smallest balances first or the ones with the highest interest rates and most injurious long-term effects.

- Stop purchasing items using credit: use cash or a debit card.

The Price of Getting Ahead — Power Savings

- Create an emergency fund of at least $3,000 in cash and use it only for true emergencies.

Level II: Control

- Set aside 5 percent or as much as possible of your monthly income in a high-yield savings or investment account. Begin looking ahead at retirement needs.

- Save for designated non-monthly expenses on a monthly basis to avoid capsizing your monthly budget.

6

Set the Timer

Creating Milestones,
Setting Goals

WHEN I WAS A CHILD, I ALWAYS WONDERED HOW AN OCEAN
liner could fit on the street where my family lived. Never mind
that ships sailed on water, and we lived on a small street in a
small town in northern New Jersey, nowhere near the shore.
Nonetheless, my father made constant reference to the time
when his ship would come in.

Later I learned that his figure of speech referred to a future
time when our family's financial resources would increase significantly. And until we boarded that ship, my parents insisted
that we would live within our limited means and confine our
purchases to only those items that we could afford. They were
both very responsible with finances, and their perspective did
not include incurring debt as part of our lifestyle.

When my dad died in 1975, he left very little debt behind.
Instead he left a list that described all of his business affairs —
names, account numbers, contact information, and a strategy for each fiscal relationship. The primary debt was the

mortgage on the house along with a few small bills — all covered by insurance and paid in full upon his death. My mother was forty-four when my father died and most grateful that he did not leave her burdened by debt with a stack of unpaid bills.

One would think that I inherited my passion for financial responsibility from him. Certainly, both my parents modeled a commonsense approach to finances that sustained a freedom that I never considered until I was a young adult. Like so many of us, the truth is that I learned about financial responsibility the hard way, as I shared earlier. Now as an adult who had to experience financial slavery before he could be set free, I understand and appreciate their example more than ever.

My father's ship never did come in, but we always had plenty to eat, clothes to wear, and a nice roof over our heads. If we were lacking some essential luxuries, I was not aware of it. However, I did learn to appreciate the incredible, priceless gift my parents gave me, once I married and started my own family. My father and mother were financially free people, and they modeled a commonsense lifestyle grounded in the truth of my father's old, faded leather Bible. Our ships can come in if we make a commitment to debt-free living and teach our children how to manage money and invest in their futures. All that's required is a little time and a lot of patience.

Reclaiming Your Future

In several earlier chapters, we've looked at the way shortsightedness, impulse purchases, and immediate gratification short-circuit our attempts at becoming financially responsible and solvent. Understandably, when we already feel discouraged and depressed over our finances, it can be tempting to give in to the short view and live for only today. It can be tempting to live in denial about the fact that we alone are responsible for our financial freedom. This is why so many people fall prey to get-rich-quick schemes and the allure of playing the lottery or gambling. However, these measures do not contribute to our commitment to dfree® living; they merely sustain our illusions and postpone the end of our enslavement to debt.

God calls us to live in the present even as we keep our minds and hearts on eternity. This duality applies to our finances as well. We must accept our present reality and take responsibility for how we got to this point. However, we must also look to the future and move into the freedom that comes from being grounded in our relationship with Christ.

Understanding the relationship between time and money is crucial if you are to break the shackles of debt and experience dfree® living. Two proverbial clichés come to mind that nonetheless convey that relationship. The first is something you've probably heard all your life, especially from managers, employers, and nagging parents: "Time *is* money." This principle forms the foundation for virtually every lending institution, credit card company, financial organization, or corporate business. These entities count on the fact that they will make money over time.

Perhaps the easiest, most unsettling examples are the payday loan companies that continue to pop up around every corner and in every strip mall in most American cities. While the methodology may vary, the fundamentals are the same. The company loans you the amount you want to borrow against your next paycheck, usually scheduled for you to receive within thirty days. But they charge you their percentage (which may not even include their "handling fee," "holding fee," or "documents charge").

So let's say an emergency comes up and you need to borrow $1,000 against your next month's salary. You agree to pay the payday loan agency $1,150 on the date your paycheck arrives. Many agencies even have you write them a check on your account, postdating it to the future payday. This practice is illegal, since knowingly writing a check without sufficient funds to cover it is against the law. This matter aside, what should be against the law is charging what amounts to over 390 percent annual interest on a loan! Before you get out your calculator to check my math, think about the reality of this amount. It's tempting to think that you're only paying 15 percent interest ($150 on $1,000), which is exorbitant enough. However, when you realize that you're paying this amount twice per month, the truth sinks in. If you paid this amount of interest every two weeks for an entire year, the amount of annual interest plus fees would exceed 500 percent! It's sheer craziness and you don't want to let your emergency be someone else's windfall.

While reputable banks and other lending institutions practice more scrupulous methods, they still rely on the fact that they can give customers something now and in return get something-plus-interest over a longer period of time. They're aware that people will pay more over the long run for immediate access to the money they need now. When we succumb to their services, we are basically placing a mortgage on our future. When we cannot meet our obligations to repay what we owe, then it feels like our future has been foreclosed. If we're going to achieve debt-free living, we must learn to turn the tables and make time work for us.

Time Is Money

Just as banks and credit card companies make money off of the amounts we borrow or finance with them, we can make money from banks and investment institutions by receiving interest when we allow them to hold our money in their accounts. Depending on the interest rate at which we're paid and the amount of time for which we commit our money to remain in a particular account, we can make the same kind of profit as any of the lenders to whom we're indebted.

Consider, for example, how much money you will accumulate over your working lifetime (say from age thirty to sixty-five) if you put $200 in a compound-interest savings account each month. Over the course of that thirty-five-year time period, at 3 percent you would end up with $148,680 at age sixty-five. If your yield was at 6 percent compounded each month as you continue to build into it, then your result would be $286,370. If you were fortunate enough to find a high-interest account that paid you 12 percent compounded monthly, then at age sixty-five you would be a millionaire! The yield would be approximately $1.3 million. No wonder Albert Einstein said, "Compound interest is the most powerful force in the universe."

There's a corollary to the notion that time is money, called the Rule of 72. In finance, the Rule of 72 is a down and dirty layperson's guide to calculating the length of time it takes to double your money in an investment. For example, if you place your money in an account at 4 percent interest, then it will take roughly eighteen years to double your investment (72 ÷ 4% = 18 years). If your rate of return is 6 percent, then your investment doubles in about twelve years. At 12 percent, you'll have twice as much as what you started with in six years.

While it's not precise, the Rule of 72 gives you a rough estimate of how much money you'll make in interest in a given time period. As disappointing or disconcerting as it may be, I encourage you to do the math and determine how many doubling periods you have left in your lifetime. If it's late in your career and your professional earning power has reached a plateau, then you may want to invest in a more aggressive, but still sound, investment fund. If you're fairly young and at the front end of your earning power, then you can afford a slower rate of return (often in exchange for having more immediate access to your investment).

Yes, it's true that "time is money," but also realize that money is *not* time. Our finances may go up and down depending on the economy, our particular career, our spending habits, and whether or not we inherit a large windfall. As so many of us found out when the recession hit, we can lose thousands, even millions, of dollars overnight as investment values plummet and stocks hit rock bottom. Everything can literally change on a dime.

However, while money comes and goes, time passes and can never be regained. Time, along with our health, is truly one of our most precious commodities. God has given us the gift of life on this earth for a set period of time, and he wants us to make the most of it. Never attempt to use money to solve a problem for which time is the only answer — either time that needs to be spent with another person or time that needs to be spent alone in reflection, contemplation, or mourning.

Time Flies

Just as time has worked against you when you didn't count the future cost of immediate gratification, it can now motivate you to make the most of each and every day. If you're willing to work with it instead of against it, time can truly be on your side as you reclaim your financial freedom. Perhaps the best way to change your perspective on time is to realize the constancy of its passing. We have twenty-four hours in every day, seven days in every week, and 365 days in every year. Time stops for no one. Only God is not subject to its progression.

Regardless of how bad is your situation or how devastating your loss, regardless of how wonderful is your life or how amazing things seem to be, time passes at the same rate for all of us. As corny as it may sound, if you want to reclaim your freedom from financial slavery, then never overlook that each morning is a gift from God, with new mercies from him that are as fresh as the dew on a spring day.

We're reminded of this truth consistently throughout the Bible, particularly in the Psalms and Proverbs. "As for man, his days are like grass, he flourishes like a flower," writes the psalmist (103:15). Or consider the way the prophet Isaiah contrasts the temporal nature of our life here on earth with the eternal, timeless constant of God and His Word:

> All flesh is grass,
> and all its beauty is like the flower of the field.
> The grass withers, the flower fades
> when the breath of the LORD blows on it;
> surely the people are grass.

Level II: Control

The grass withers, the flower fades,
but the word of our God will stand forever.
Isaiah 40:6–8 ESV

So often we become caught up in the pressures of today that we fail to appreciate each day as a gift from God. Just as time can work for us in making money, we must realize that our current economic woes will pass. The God who created the universe gives us a gift far more precious than any amount of money, riches, or earthly treasure. He gives us bodily life through our parents at the time of our birth, and He gives us eternal life through the body of His Son Jesus, which was broken on the cross for us before being raised up again on the third day.

As we consider the fleeting nature of our lives and how quickly our lives seem to accelerate as we get older, we must use our time as wisely as possible, especially regarding the resources with which we've been entrusted. Jesus tells the story of a wealthy man who had to go out of town for an extended period. So he went to his top three lieutenants and gave each of them a portion of his wealth to manage while he was away. The first captain received five different accounts to manage; the second one was given three accounts; and the third was given one to oversee.

When the wealthy man returned, he met with each of his three leaders to get an update on his accounts. His first two captains both gave exceptional reports: they invested what he gave them and had consequently doubled his money. However, the third leader, who had been given only one account to manage, handed over the same account balance as when his boss had given it to him. "Knowing what a shrewd, strict businessman you are," the overseer explained, "I kept the account on reserve so that I wouldn't lose any money while you were away."

You don't have to watch Donald Trump on *The Apprentice* to know the wealthy man's response: "You're fired! You wicked, lazy man — I'm so disappointed in you! You could at least have invested this and turned some kind of profit instead of sitting on it and making excuses. Get out of my sight — go!" His rebuke is sharp, heightened all the more by his warm congratulatory promotions of his first two captains: "Well done, gentlemen! You've increased the assets with which you were invested so you're ready for more responsibility with greater assets."

God holds us accountable for far more than how much we owe on our credit card balances. And he's not storming around heaven, pacing back and forth, waiting to come down on us when we fail. No, he simply knows what we're capable of doing and wants us to discover that purpose and thrive at it. He wants us to invest the time we've been given in eternal pursuits, not in just the frivolous, feel-good pursuits of a prodigal son or daughter. The good news is that it's never too late to start investing wisely, both in ourselves and with our resources.

Most of us don't plan to fail with regard to our finances. No one sets out to be irresponsible so they wind up burdened by the pressure of living paycheck to paycheck, behind on bills for items they no longer enjoy or even remember. No, we don't plan to fail; we merely fail to plan. It's not too late. If you've made it this far in the book, then you're clearly serious about making serious changes in pursuit of your financial freedom.

Now is the time to get serious and make the most of the time you have. Pay attention to financial payment deadlines.

Level II: Control

Set concrete goals with specific time lines and target dates even if those numbers on the calendar seem so far into the future that you can't imagine it. As you'll see in the next chapter, once you begin to see the progress you're making, then you can really increase your momentum. As you begin paying off some of your debt, you then have more income to devote to your remaining debt. Set the timer, my friend, for your time is now!

Get

AHEAD

"Several years ago, we bought into the concepts of dfree® and began implementing them in our lives. We were holding our own and didn't consider ourselves in financial 'slavery' until we looked ahead and realized we hadn't really planned very far in advance, for emergencies, or retirement, or anything. Upon recently finding out that both of our current jobs will be ending December 31 of this year, my wife and I are in a far better position financially to deal with an unforeseeable future as it relates to our career futures.

"The notion of being dfree® —no debt, no delinquencies, no deficits—is even more real when one's immediate future holds the prospect of being without jobs. We haven't panicked and know that we will weather this season of our lives with the help of the dfree® principles we've learned and continue to practice."

David and Carrie T., Hillsborough, NJ

7

Maximize the Margin

Saving and Investing,
Building Wealth

I ONCE TAUGHT A COURSE ON RACE RELATIONS AT A COMMU-
nity college. During our discussions over the semester, it
became clear that my African American students believed
that the United States government had a special program that
helped Asian immigrants start their own businesses by providing them start-up capital. How else, my students thought, could
so many Asian immigrants enter the country, speak very little,
if any, English, and become the owners of strategically located
businesses in predominantly black neighborhoods? The only
logical conclusion in my students' minds was that the government had to be making this happen. So I invited a young
Asian businessman who had done that very thing — bought a
business on a prime corner in a black neighborhood — to be a
guest speaker in my class.

What my students heard shocked them. This young man
had come from his country to America with $13. He lived
in an apartment with some relatives who had already moved

here. He slept on the floor. He worked in their business and spent very little money. He owned two shirts, one pair of black pants, one pair of shoes, underwear, and a few other accessory items. After saving most of his income, he joined a monthly group of a dozen people, who had also emigrated from his country, for something they called a *ki*. This meeting was a kind of investment group that would put a certain amount of money in a pot once a month, and each month one person would take all of the money. The next month person number two would take the money. And so on. This would happen for the number of months that equaled the number of people in the group. And then they would start a new group.

This young man wanted to buy a business that required $30,000 in cash. So he joined a group of fifteen people who put in $2,000 every month. He could afford this high investment because, despite his low salary, he saved virtually everything he earned. And when his turn came, he took his $30,000 and bought his business. My students wanted to know how he could trust this system to work. Suppose someone did not show up the next month? There were no contracts, no paperwork, no credit checks, no government oversight. It was an honor system, and this, he said, was a part of his culture.

Community Support

This example illustrates two very important aspects of the way the dfree® program works. First, the young man I brought in to talk with my class planned his work and then worked his plan. He had no government grant, no wealthy venture capitalist backing his dream, and no personal wealth from which to draw. In fact, by most of our standards, he would be considered below the poverty level and might be presumed to be the least likely to succeed. Obviously, however, this was not the case.

In the pursuit of financial freedom, I do not think there's an advantage for any race or ethnicity over another. I do believe that for many individuals raised in a different culture, it may be easier to sacrifice and do the hard work of saving and living within one's means. Their previous culture may not have "spoiled" them as much as our own does with its emphasis on convenience and comfort, status and luxury. They also accept the fact that they must rely on a community of support if they are to be successful. This is the second significant lesson we can learn from his example.

We can see the significance of a supportive community in virtually every recovery program and therapeutic approach. From the classic 12-step model of Alcoholics Anonymous to the friendly approach of Weight Watchers, anyone who has experienced a dramatic change from a negative, harmful lifestyle to a positive, healthy way of living knows this truth. You will not be able to maximize your financial freedom until you develop a group with which you can share your present financial realities and your future dreams of freedom, your struggles as well as your victories.

As I've mentioned, for our dfree® movement, the church provided this organic community of individuals with a common problem and a shared solution. While I've alluded to the fact that you must identify and collaborate with another person for the sake of accountability, I cannot stress enough the difference it makes to have a group encouraging you and sharing your journey along the way. Like any area in which we struggle, particularly one as personal as money, it's challenging at first to be transparent and vulnerably share the truth. What has amazed me is that we read in the papers or online in the news every day that millions of us are burdened by debt, and yet everyone feels isolated and alone in their own financial prison cell. If you haven't already assembled a support network — more than just one person with whom you're sharing your dfree® commitments — then I challenge you to make that your next priority.

If you're uncomfortable speaking directly with family and friends, or you know that they will not encourage and support your new changes, then you will have to make new acquaintances. Oddly enough, it can often be easier to build community to overcome a problem if there's no prior relationship or personal history. If nothing else, I hope that this book will provide a catalyst for individuals to come together and discuss the dfree® principles and recommendations. You could simply post a notice, either online or on your church bulletin board or community center window, saying that you're starting a book discussion group aimed at improving one's financial health. Such a group could facilitate looking at a variety of materials, not just dfree®, that could nourish and sustain the group's motivation.

The Price of Prosperity

Another barrier to maximizing your success that is addressed in the dfree® program has to do with one's attitude toward wealth. So far we've examined some of the ways our culture reinforces affluence, wealth, and riches — assuming that we all view these as positives. Interestingly enough, many Christians often have a backlash reaction that impedes their receptivity to getting ahead. Many of their negative ideas on wealth are tied to the story of the young man who visited Jesus asking what he must do to have eternal life. It's usually referred to as the story of the "rich young ruler" and can be found in Luke 18:18–25.

Jesus responds to the young man's question by exploring the man's notion of what it means to be "good" and by emphasizing the importance of keeping God's commandments. When the young man replies that he has kept God's commandments since boyhood, Jesus tells him that there's then only one thing he can do: "Sell everything you have and give to the poor, and you will have treasure in heaven. Then come, follow me" (Luke 18:22). Apparently not what the young man had hoped to hear, since his response is described as being "very sad" because he had "great wealth" (v. 23).

Seeing the young man's crestfallen response — and this is where many Christians point — Jesus says, "How hard it is for the rich to enter the kingdom of God! Indeed, it is easier for a camel to go through the eye of a needle than for [someone who is] rich ... to enter the kingdom of God" (vv. 24–25). But Christ goes on to explain that it's not impossible, since all things are possible with His heavenly Father, and that, ultimately, anyone who gives up everything for God's kingdom will receive back more than it was worth many times over.

The rationale behind Christ's response — because it's clear He is not condemning rich people here — is that being wealthy makes it more difficult to need help, need other people, and ultimately to need God. If we can go out and afford to buy anything we want, then we're probably not praying about them and relying directly on God to provide them. Instead, we're focused on our latest purchase, insuring it, renting a storage unit for it, and wondering why it's taking so long for the next version to come out. The more we have, the more tempted we are to cling to material possessions as idols. As Jesus explains in a different conversation, "What good will it be for [someone to gain] the whole world, yet forfeit [their] soul? Or what can [anyone] give in exchange for [their] soul?" (Matthew 16:26).

When we can attain what we want ourselves, then we've added a layer that often obscures how desperately we truly need God. The only thing holy about being in debt is that we eventually have nowhere to turn, or no one to turn to, who can help except our Father. Slaves brought to this country in the early stages of our country's development knew that they had no hope of freedom except a divine hope. They naturally relied on spirituals and hymns to express their desperate plea for freedom to God. Similarly, we must turn to the one source who can truly guide us to freedom, both spiritually and financially.

And as we grow in both kinds of freedom, there's nothing to fear in becoming successful or even wealthy. Nothing in the Bible causes me to conclude that a Christian cannot have wealth. Jesus did warn against the potential distraction and obstruction that wealth could represent (Luke 12:15–21). But nowhere did Jesus teach that we should not be wealthy at all. In fact Jesus' ministry attracted some very wealthy people and He was the recipient of some very fine gifts from the time He was born (Matthew 2:1–2, 11).

When He was anointed with very expensive oil that had been contained in an equally expensive jar, Jesus rebuked those who criticized the extravagance (Mark 14:3–9). The grave that Jesus conquered on Easter Sunday morning was owned by a rich man named Joseph who donated his gravesite to the cause (Mark 15:42–47).

Wealth is a blessing from God, and there is nothing in the dfree® movement that condemns wealth. True riches accumulate, however, from the sheer joy of experiencing and maintaining debt-free living: we pay as we go, pay our bills on time, and live within our means. No longer burdened by the slavery of consumer debt, we are unleashed to share the riches of God's love and the wisdom of His Word with everyone around us.

Full-Throttle Payments

For many of us, getting out of debt and accumulating wealth may seem a long way off. Nevertheless, we must not fear our success and allow it to impede our progress. As we begin to see progress made in our behaviors, as we begin to watch account balances decrease each month, as our confidence and enthusiasm in new habits grow, we must then use this momentum to go "full throttle." Let me explain.

From assessing the details of your current financial situation and developing your spending plan, I want you to go back through the items that will be paid off in the next year, the next two years, and the next three years. It may be your car loan, the outstanding balance on a department store credit card, or the remaining debt from your school loans. Based on your schedule of payments, however, these are all relatively finite expenses that will soon be paid off in full. Take this list and look at the amount of each one's monthly payment. Once they are paid off, if you take the same money that you had been applying to each of these accounts and apply it to one of your high-interest debts, you will begin to experience the power of having time on your side.

Experts such as Dave Ramsey call this the "snowball" method because you're using your successes to accumulate more power in paying off the remaining debt you owe. Financial guru Suze Orman takes a similar approach with her online tool called the "Debt Eliminator." Regardless of what we call it, you will find it requires considerable discipline to maintain focus. Because after you have paid off a few of your debts, you will begin to discover some new room to maneuver financially.

Most credit card companies do not want you to have a zero balance, since they ultimately lose money on soft costs such as mailing statements and promotions. In the prosperity of the 1990s into the new millennium, when someone paid off a credit card balance, the company would often increase that person's credit limit and lower the annual percentage rate. I surmise their strategy was to encourage card carriers to splurge on a large-item purchase — a vacation, major appliance, or luxury status item such as a fur coat or new watch. These days, credit card companies often penalize those who maintain a zero balance.

One of my credit card companies contacted me recently to inform me that since I do not use my card on a consistent basis, they were reducing my credit limit from $12,000 to $1,000. This news did not bother me at all — in fact, I was grateful for the lower threshold of temptation should I be swayed to consider using it. There's both a dark side and a silver lining to the ruthless way most credit card companies and lenders responded during the Great Recession. They finally cracked down on their delinquent users, in some ways making it a fall-or-fly push out of the comfortable nest of consumer credit use. This may feel harsh at first but ultimately assists the delinquents in obtaining their freedom.

One dfree® participant told me that the best thing that ever happened to her was when American Express canceled her credit card. She was behind in her payments and had been slow in contacting them and explaining how and when she would be catching up. So after dozens of ignored voice messages and emails from American Express, this woman discovered that her card had been canceled. While she was still responsible for the balance she owed (and would be paying on for several years, apparently), she could no longer perpetuate the cycle by using the card to charge more.

Some dfree® participants told me that after they paid off the balance on their credit cards and established enough savings to use as an emergency cushion, they called their credit card companies and requested that their credit limits be lowered. While the wisdom of this tactic may vary from situation to situation and the terms of the company, it's a true sign of growth when you find yourself taking proactive steps to limit your spending and attain your freedom.

Let's review what it means to maximize the margin of your success once you've started your dfree® quest. First, you must ensure that you have ongoing support for the rest of the long road ahead, and you must be willing to ask for help appropriately when you need it. Next, you must examine your feelings on your new first steps of success. How would you feel about yourself if you not only regained your financial freedom but actually accumulated wealth? Accept that this will become your reality and anticipate how to maintain focus, which we will cover shortly.

Finally, as you begin to pay off some of your debt, use the percentage of your income that you had been devoting to those payments toward the remaining debt. Resist the temptation to return to old habits or celebrate with a splurge purchase. Instead, focus on how it feels to breathe the fresh air of financial mobility as you remove some of the many chains that bind you. Relish your strength and commit to using your growing power to break the shackles of financial slavery forever. You can do it!

8

Minimize the Stress

Buying Insurance,
Planning Wills/Estates

I ONCE LOST AN ELECTION BECAUSE I AM BLACK. ALTHOUGH this statement accurately sums up my experience, it's obviously more complicated than it sounds. As a sixteen-year-old junior at a New Jersey suburban high school, I decided that I had a chance at the end of my high school career to run for president of the student body. I was not a newcomer to student affairs at my school. I had served as treasurer of my junior class, was a fairly popular athlete, was already active in student government, and had a diverse group of friends — both black and white. A large group of them encouraged me to run, and the competition didn't seem particularly formidable.

We believed we could get a substantial number of white votes since our school did not suffer a tremendous racial problem. To the extent that we may have had some white students who simply would not vote for a black candidate, we believed that they were definitely in the minority. After all, a black man was running for mayor of our predominantly white town and, in that same year, he would win the election. So it was reasonable to believe that the students would be at least as open in their thinking as their parents were. Also, we knew we would get major support from the black students. This was the 1960s — social change and black pride were in the air. We had a winning formula.

We organized our campaign committee, and it was well-represented by cheerleaders — the school's best-looking girls. We created campaign posters and other materials. We even had campaign buttons; that was big stuff for a high school campaign in those days. All indications were that I would become only the second African American elected to lead the student body and the first one in many years.

When Election Day arrived, we discovered that the majority of black students were barred from voting. The facts surrounding the reason for these students being unable to vote has influenced my work and my life to this very day. Here is what happened.

Our high school was adamant about preparing us for the real world in every conceivable way. That included the manner in which the school conducted student government elections. The school actually rented real voting machines — the same machines used by our parents in presidential elections. And the school required that we register to vote in student government elections just as our parents had to register to vote in presidential elections. Students were given this information beforehand: some received it during freshman orientation; others got it in our student handbooks at the start of the school year.

Somehow I had gotten this information too and had registered without even remembering exactly when I did it. Apparently almost all of the white students were registered also. But the overwhelming majority of the black students — we had no

Hispanic or Asian students in our school — not only had not registered to vote, they were not even aware that they were supposed to register. After the election results and the news of so many black students being turned away from voting, our first thought was that there had to be a white culprit who was stopping a black student — namely, me — from becoming president of a predominantly white student government. The situation had to have race-related injustice at the core.

However, it didn't take long to conclude that this speculation actually made little or no sense. How could anyone have managed to stage a racially motivated conspiracy of this nature and keep it quiet? The school would never stand for it, nor would the students. Nonetheless, I struggled to know the best way to respond to such a devastating loss that could have been so easily prevented.

In that sense, we were in a tricky situation. Some sort of racial analysis could have been done to evaluate the situation and prove that the dominant culture had performed inadequately in embracing and encouraging the black students' participation in school-wide elections. We probably could have constructed an articulate position on the inherent likelihood of black students being disinterested in voting due to past discrimination and therefore argued that affirmative steps should have been taken to ameliorate the historic underrepresentation of blacks in student government.

In other words, I am certain that I could have made a passionate speech about how the white power structure should have known better, and when they saw the disparity in racial composition of students who were and were not registered to vote, they should have nullified the results and created a more just and fair process. I could easily have charged the school officials' failings as racist, described the black students as victims, and even accused the system of having permanently ruined my political prospects for life.

After all, had I won the election, I might have gone on to become an elected official in my state. I could have been the first black president of the United States! This racial analysis could have concluded that my entire life had been victimized and limited. I could have concluded that it was all the fault of my racist, insensitive high school!

Instead my friends and I chose to respond by deciding that never again would the black students in our school miss any important information and absent themselves from any meaningful activity. We recognized that this issue of registering and voting represented a disturbing pattern of de facto segregation within an integrated institution, and we had to organize an effort that would insure that we were full participants at the school. We could not determine how intentionally exclusive the registration policy was and did not know whether the policy's aim was suppression of black student participation — nor did that matter very much. The results spoke for themselves, and since the school officials did not seem to be overwhelmed with concern about the results, we decided to fix the problem ourselves.

We formed an organization at the school whose goal was to make sure every black student had every shred of information they needed to participate fully in everything the school had to offer. We had to fight for the right to have such a group, but we won the fight and did our work.

Forty years later, I find myself thinking exactly as I did when I was sixteen. I spend less of my time fighting to prove what caused the problems in our culture and more of my time working to offer solutions for the many challenges, responsibilities, and opportunities with which we are presented. My personal motto is this: "The only thing worse than not having what you need is not using what you have."

Begin with the End

I tell this story because the collective impact of multiple individuals not knowing that they had to register or simply not registering despite knowing created a huge impact on the outcome. Too often, participants in our dfree® movement are not fully aware of the impact their ignorance or indifference can have on the final season of their lives. If you're not attending to the details of your financial future, if you're not realizing the consequences that will transpire based on your lack of action, then you've set yourself up for a lifetime of financial slavery.

Let me share an example of what can happen when we don't pay attention to what's required of us. Our work at First Baptist Church has included operating a Family Resource Center where we help families overcome barriers to self-sufficiency that have kept them stuck for many years. In one case a woman got a parking ticket that she either could not or did not pay. The ticket was less than $20. Because she did not pay the parking violation, a warrant was issued for her arrest, and her driver's license and car registration were suspended.

Shortly thereafter, the local police recognized that her license plates matched the plates of a car on the suspended list, and when they stopped her, they realized she was driving without a valid driver's license. They towed her car and gave her a new summons to appear in court. By the time this comedy of errors completely unfolded, along with a few more infractions of the motor vehicle laws, this woman had no car, no license, and no transportation to get to her job. Not surprising, she then lost her job and had no ability to pay her rent since she had lost her job. She ended up homeless — and this all began with a parking ticket that could have been resolved for less than $20. It took us more than five years to help get her back on track with her life.

It's not always a matter of something we've ignored. Sometimes the issue that causes real disaster is having insufficient insurance on a car or apartment or home or a life. Sometimes it is a family member dying and having no will to define the distribution of assets. This can be prevented and should be a high priority in your dfree® strategy. Our lives consist of so many interconnected parts that one of them can affect all of them. One of the key connectors is our future financial capacity and what will happen when we can no longer work or when we're no longer here.

Defining Your Retirement

Hard hit by the recession and unemployment, so many people have been forced to take a premature distribution from their 401(k) retirement account. While such action is not desirable and should be a last resort, obviously desperate times call for desperate measures. Whether borrowing from or depleting your retirement account is preferable to borrowing more money is debatable. If it's a short-term loan that you have a plan for repaying, and it's at a reasonable rate of interest that's comparable to the interest rate of your retirement or savings account, then borrowing money may be acceptable.

The frightening impact for so many people remains that they have no emergency fund to fall back on, either short-term or long-term. Whether you're in your twenties and just embarking on your journey in the workforce or in your sixties and on the descent of your professional career, everyone must have a plan for their retirement. If, like many people I know, you say, "Well, I'm never going to retire because I enjoy my work," then that's wonderful. Nonetheless, your earning power will not always be where it is today, nor will the cost of your health care. You must plan for the future as if your life depends on it. Because it does — no one else is going to take care of you the way you are.

One way to go about it is to consider your present lifestyle and how it compares to the lifestyle you would like to have at retirement age. It's one thing to downsize from the nice home you're in now because the kids are grown, but it's another to be forced to downsize into something you don't want or like simply because it's all you can afford. Most experts recommend that you should assume needing at least 80 percent of your current income to live on when you retire. You may think you can get by on a lot less if you have to, but the older we get, the more resistant to change most of us get as well.

Perhaps a better place to start is to back up and think through your definition of retirement. If you're simply viewing it as the day "when your ship comes in" and you can quit the job you've despised for most of your career, then you're in for a rude awakening. If you don't like your job and find your career field unsatisfying, then retirement is not the solution. You need to get honest with yourself and think through what it is that you really love doing and consider how to make a living doing it. Retirement is best thought of as a season when you have more choices of how to spend your time because you have the security of enough money to live on comfortably (not extravagantly, but comfortably).

If you didn't have to go to work and you didn't have to be concerned about having adequate financial security, then how would you spend your time? Would you travel and see exotic locales that you've always dreamed of visiting? Would you take up golf, or swimming, or gardening? Maybe write that book you've always wanted to write or spend more time with your grandkids? Perhaps coach a Little League team or assist with hospitality at your church? We'll touch on these again in the next level on giving back, but it's important to have some specific ideas of how you want to spend your life in a later season.

Unfortunately, for many us, growing older has not meant growing wiser financially. In the past decade, the number of bankruptcies declared by people sixty-five and older increased over 150 percent! Or consider the results of a *USA Today* survey in which more than half of the participants surveyed — all of them sixty-five or older — were still working because they had to work in order to survive. Do you really want to have to work at McDonalds or Walmart at the end of your life? And the sad reality is that, despite federal restrictions on age discrimination, many people cannot maintain their present jobs indefinitely. Many senior citizens in our country are forced to take minimum-wage jobs in order to supplement their Social Security just to scrape by.

Now is the time to purpose the kind of retirement you want to live. Be realistic about what's likely to happen and be honest about what you'd like to have happen. Do not get caught in a fantasy world of winning the lottery or becoming a Vegas card shark. Many people harbor the fantasy that their standard of living will go up once they retire, while the data consistently reveal that the standard of living drops significantly for the vast majority of Americans.

It may help if you think of someone who models the kind of retirement you'd like to have. They shouldn't necessarily be wealthy — in fact, it's probably better if they're not — but they should clearly be controlling their time and doing what they love doing the most. They should appear to be loving life and contributing love and support to their families, churches, and communities without the burdens of financial slavery inhibiting them. If possible, initiate a conversation with such a person and tell them you admire the way they're living and wonder if they could share some of what they've learned. You might be surprised at what you learn that you can implement before it's too late.

The key to a successful retirement is threefold: (1) to have a retirement fund to which you contribute each month, (2) to have a specific goal — an actual dollar amount — that you have set as your retirement target, and (3) to imagine what you want your later years in life to look like and to take the necessary steps now to begin making it happen.

Will Power

While it's not pleasant to consider, perhaps the most crucial part of planning for your retirement and beyond is making sure you have a written will. If you don't have a will, it is possible your estate will be divided by the government. Your spouse and children may or may not get what you intended for them to have because your estate will end up in probate, which allows for virtually anyone you've ever encountered to make a claim on it. In addition, your family may experience significant tension and conflict as they try to make decisions about what you have left behind. Estate planners report that as many as 70 percent of Americans each year die without having a will in place.

Insurance

Naturally, as part of your planning process, you will want to consider life insurance. The Bible tells us, "A good man leaves an inheritance for his children's children" (Proverbs 13:22). As a pastor for most of my adult life, I cannot tell you how many funerals I've performed or how many families I've seen who had their grief compounded because their loved one left them with a financial mess — no will, no life insurance, lots of debts. While it may be tempting (albeit selfishly) to think that your adult children can pay for your funeral and burial expenses after you're gone, this is often not possible. Unfortunately, parents who think this way often instill similar short-sighted, and irresponsible, habits in their children.

I recently had to face one of the hardest parts of my job in just such a situation. A lady in our congregation died, and her four adult children could not afford to bury her, so they came to me to ask if the church would pay her funeral and burial costs. As we discussed the situation, it was clear that the four siblings had exhausted other possibilities and avenues of provision. They were each in so much debt, with maxed-out credit cards that would not hold additional charges at the grocery store, let alone the funeral home, that they were up against a wall.

As much as I wanted to help them and allow the church to pay for their mother's burial expenses, I had to tell them no. It sounds terribly callous and cold-hearted, but the reality of the situation is this. In order to serve everyone in our church equally and fairly, we would have to be willing to pay for any member's burial. At its most inexpensive, a burial or cremation runs between $3,000 and $5,000. Considering that our church holds funerals and memorial services for around 350 people a year, we would quickly go bankrupt if we paid for every one of them to be buried.

It was heart-wrenching for me as a pastor to make this decision and share it with this already grieving family. But it would have been irresponsible of me as a pastor and leader to make an exception. We all know we're going to die someday. If you truly want to minimize stress in your life, then having the security of knowing that your debts will not be left for your spouse or children to clean up can be more than a worthwhile investment.

Leaving a sum of money for your family and beneficiaries ensures that losing your income will not cause undue hardship on them. Your survivors can maintain the same quality of life that you had provided for them. You not only want to leave them with a legacy of integrity, love, and faith, but you want to leave them financially secure enough to pursue their own dreams and adjust to life without you.

Like many of the other financial components we've discussed, life insurance raises many considerations, and my best advice is for you to talk to a trusted and qualified estate planner or licensed insurance agent. There are good reasons to choose different types of life insurance, but this is an issue that needs to be discussed between you and a qualified professional whom you trust.

Some financial experts encourage you to take out a policy that pays ten times your present annual salary. Then you have the security of knowing your debts will be paid and your family will be provided for. The payout is usually dramatically higher than what you've paid in premiums. A policy that pays ten times your annual salary may be more than you can afford as you begin your dfree® transformation, so find a policy that you can afford and then review it each year to see if you can increase coverage as you reduce debt.

Another formula for calculating how much life insurance you need is called the "DIME" — Debt, Income, Mortgage, Education — method. It's simply the sum of your outstanding debt, income replacement for your family and survivors, the balance of your mortgage, and the approximate cost of your children's college education.

As you continue to make great strides toward your financial freedom, you will want to include retirement and estate planning in your comprehensive strategy. Such a component provides a concrete financial provision for you and your family years from now while providing the priceless intangible benefit of present peace of mind. The goal of dfree® living is to maximize your mastery over your finances while simultaneously minimizing stress related to money-related matters.

9

Maintain the Focus

Ongoing Accountability,
Celebrating Your Success

I'VE ALREADY SHARED MY WEAKNESS FOR BEAUTIFUL NECKTIES, so it likely comes as no surprise that I also love a well-made suit. Like most professional men, whether they admit it or not, I like looking my best and having the confidence that comes from wearing a stylish, beautifully cut suit of clothes. I succumb to vanity just as much as the next person when it comes to wanting others to view me as successful, professional, fashionable, and well groomed.

My love of suits is a bit ironic since I didn't own a suit — not one — when I entered my professional career in a very public role. I came into the ministry through the side door and had never considered myself a preacherish kind of person. I wore blue jeans and sneakers, had a big Afro, and, frankly, I felt fine about it since my boss dressed the same way. People would invite me to speak at large banquets where the other guests wore tuxedos and gowns, and I would say to myself, *I don't have to dress like them. I'm going as I am.* I never felt like anything was wrong with me because that's who I was. And as we've seen, this is a good thing because significance does not come from the outside. It comes from inside, knowing who God created us to be.

While I know the source of my significance better now than I did then, I have come to enjoy nice suits and have struggled with a dilemma. I've reached a point in my financial freedom that allows me to purchase any new suit I want while still maintaining my dfree® lifestyle. The problem is that I have almost a dozen nice suits hanging in my closet with absolutely nothing wrong with them. The only features distinguishing them from a new one would be whether or not the pants are cuffed or have a plain finish or perhaps a slight difference in the width of the jacket's lapels — something like one-eighth to one-fourth inch. These little details are usually the only things that indicate how up-to-date a man is in his suit fashion.

While this is an ongoing temptation, I have to tell you that I simply cannot justify buying a new suit just because the ones I own reflect details from a few seasons ago. As my friends have reminded me, who really notices those small details on a man's suit? I know that I'm probably the only person who notices the difference. If I were replacing a worn-out old suit or had a hole in my wardrobe for a particular kind of suit, it would be one thing. But I don't. So I'm resisting the urge to buy a new suit.

When Greed Becomes "Good"

My main reason for confessing my sartorial weakness is to illustrate the importance of maintaining dfree® principles once you can afford to loosen your spending habits. As you begin to experience more and more freedom from the financial slavery that once bound you so tightly, you may be inclined to revert to old habits. You may feel like you're a little bit better than most people since you've reduced your debts and can afford to charge more than many of your friends and coworkers. But if you're not paying attention and remaining focused, it can be a quick slide back into the pit out of which you have worked so hard to climb.

This tendency can be avoided if you remain anchored by the biblical principles of dfree® living. But as we've seen, so many factors and forces conspire against us in our culture. What our culture has come to accept as tolerable or even desirable runs counter to serving as good stewards of God's resources. Without getting on my cultural soapbox, consider just a few of the cultural values that we now take for granted, even consider to be "good."

Foremost, we now battle the blatant assumption that everyone wants more money, that you can't have too much, and that you'll do whatever it takes to have as much as possible. In his book *The Spirit of Democratic Capitalism*, Michael Novak writes, "Democratic capitalism ... cannot thrive apart from the moral culture that nourishes the virtues and values on which its existence depends." This moral culture, according to Novak, rests upon principles that include "moral constraint." The opposite of moral constraint, or restraint, is an uninhibited gluttony, an insatiable appetite for more and more regardless of cost or consequence to self and others. Simply put, this is what we often identify, especially in an economic context, as "greed."

It goes without saying that greed has traditionally and historically been considered a vice, a flaw, a destructive character defect. Greedy people were considered selfish, egocentric, uncaring, and conniving. Think of a character like Mr. Potter, the villainous old man whose avarice, jealousy, and spite consistently plague Jimmy Stewart's sterling character, George Bailey, in the Christmas classic *It's a Wonderful Life.*

Now think about how far we've come as represented by another iconic film character: Gordon Gekko in *Wall Street.* Michael Douglas won an Academy Award for portraying a hyper-driven, unscrupulous Wall Street executive who combines his keen instincts for success in the financial markets with a ruthless, capitalism-justified greed. Douglas's character, Gordon Gekko, justifies his behavior by redefining his vice in one of the most famous movie lines of modern times: "Greed ... is good."

This cinematic depiction of moral unrestraint — greed — celebrates a cultural shift from our country's roots of honesty, restraint, and diligence. A reasonable return on investments was no longer good enough, not when so much more money can be made through deception and manipulation. Granted, many depictions of such a ruthless reversal of ethics border on hyperbole. Certainly, the carpetbaggers who exploited the South during our nation's post–Civil War reconstruction or the robber barons of early-twentieth-century industry were just as greedy as any Wall Street insider from the 1980s. Nevertheless, greed became conflated with ambition, success, and the pursuit of the American Dream, redefined as a positive motivator for anyone and everyone who desired more out of life.

During the 1990s and thereafter, greed inspired banks to offer high-interest-rate credit cards and nothing-down mortgages to people who could not afford them. Greed allowed corporations like Enron and Halliburton to dole out huge bonuses to executives while freezing wages and cutting jobs for low-wage workers. Greed spurred insider trading and other illegal practices among celebrities and government leaders.

And greed still thrives today. It motivates clothing designers to charge exorbitant prices for apparel made overseas in sweatshops and assign higher prices simply due to the presence of a logo. Greed motivates payday lenders to prey upon people of meager means, offering them access to credit that can result in repayment interest rates and fees that end up being the equivalent of 500 to 600 percent. And not all of this culture of greed resides in corporate suites.

Our culture of greed causes people to abandon family responsibilities to work more hours and earn more money to buy more things. Greed is at work when we buy more clothes than we can wear, store them in basements and attics, and then rent storage units for items we may never use again. We have replaced the cultures of modesty, sufficiency, and frugality with the culture of greed. When this spirit of greed mixes with other potent factors, our culture of debt only becomes stronger.

I'm Not a Doctor, But ...

Greed is not the only vice that has become a culturally accepted value. Our celebrity fascination and tabloid fixation reflect a culture of fantasy in which we make vicarious living and voyeuristic make-believe our everyday coping mechanism. Professor Juliet B. Schor analyzes this phenomenon with marvelous insight in her book *The Overspent American*. She asserts that in the past, striving to improve our lifestyle was not necessarily a destructive endeavor because the Joneses lived next door to us and were probably in the same income bracket with a similar lifestyle.

However, today we don't even know the Joneses that we're trying to keep up with. We're keeping up with so-called reality stars like the Kardashians and chasing every new trend that bubbles to the surface of pop culture. All too often we're idolizing film and television stars who make a lot more money than we earn and, even worse, the persona we idolize doesn't exist.

I first noticed this "fantasy as reality" phenomenon in the early 1970s when actor Robert Young starred as a fictional television doctor named Marcus Welby. In 1977 the Center for Media Literacy reported that the actor had received over a quarter million letters from viewers requesting medical advice. People were writing in to ask an actor for credible medical advice simply because he played the role of a doctor on a television show.

Robert Young became America's de facto medical expert and pitchman because people were confusing his television role with the reality of his real identity. Similarly, I have actually seen people confront television personalities from popular shows and accost them because of something their characters did on the show.

And I can be as susceptible as the next person. Retired NBA legend Julius Irving, "Dr. J," recently did a commercial in which he shoots an ice cube into a glass from across the room. As a huge fan, I loved it and excitedly told my son who was watching with me, "He could do that, you know?" When Dr. J held up a can of Dr. Pepper and said, "You know, I'm the doctor," I was suddenly thirsty.

As much as I love basketball and admire Dr. J, I don't need him telling me what to drink. He's not exactly the kind of doctor — nor is Robert Young or Marcus Welby — to advise me on what's best for my diet. But advertisers are going to use my love for his basketball to hook me into some Dr. Pepper.

This type of influence is everywhere. And it's so pervasive that it can be hard to separate what's true from what's a slick sales pitch. If we are to remain focused on our financial liberation, then we must resist the culture of celebrity that tries to manipulate us into emulation through consumption.

Flight of Fantasy

Celebrity endorsements of this kind rely on the cultural power of fantasy. Savvy marketers know this cultural illusion offers emotional comfort and psychological support for our misplaced priorities and delusional processes. Just as millions of kids really believe that they will play professional basketball and therefore do not need an education, millions of families believe that some miracle will occur that will enable them to pay bills for which they lack the money. Their purchases make them feel like they are a part of an imaginary world that they can control, and their debt fuels this illusion.

There was a time when purpose, significance, and service were celebrated as virtues worth pursuing and possessing. We have evolved into a culture of luxury that has made prosperity the god of the age. We not only admire the *Lifestyles of the Rich and Famous,* we hold them up as the standard for significance and success. We believe too that we're entitled to this standard to such a degree that we'll lie, cheat, and refuse self-accountability just so we can present ourselves as successful and prosperous.

Prosperity is often mistakenly and very narrowly defined

as simply having money and possessions. Many ministers cannot understand why they're considered "prosperity preachers" in spite of the fact that their opulent lifestyles and expensive possessions dominate their discourse. There's certainly nothing wrong with being prosperous. In fact, I devote a lot of time to helping people discover their gifts and talents, which they can use to increase their incomes. The days of graduating from school, getting a job, working there forty years, and retiring with a gold watch are long gone. Most new jobs are created by small businesses and entrepreneurship. Business ownership is going to be the way to attain prosperity for most people in the future. Let's face it – after we destroy our credit cards, pay our bills on time, and live within our means, most of us will still need more means! And every single person has an ability or skill that someone will pay them to use. There is nothing wrong with prospering financially as long as we make money and use money the right way. But a culture of prosperity results in social classifications based on possessions, purchases, and perceptions.

In our country's history, individuals used to be known by their actions or were evaluated based on their character. Today a person is known by her Louis Vuitton luggage and is evaluated based on his Rolex watch. Today we assume that people who own enough of the right possessions must be successful, smart, and sexy. If they don't, then there must be something wrong with them. But the truth is that their ability to resist cultural snares of enslavement is proof that there's likely everything right with them.

Emancipation Celebration

One of the most powerful ways to maintain focus and resist the cultural snares of greed and celebrity is to celebrate your dfree® victories along the way. As we interview participants in our church's dfree® movement, I'm amazed at how many of them emphasize the importance of our community celebrations of each other's successes. I've mentioned before that when we first started dfree®, it met with some resistance. People were reluctant to be transparent about something as personal as money, especially if it meant revealing the extent of their debt. Such vulnerability requires a level of risk that we usually do not venture into with one another.

Many of the first-time dfree® participants became more and more trusting and invested in the program as it continued. Others did not. One member told me in front of the entire choir that her money was none of my business and that this "dfree® thing" was going too far. Other resisters were not as vocal, but it was clear that we were touching some sore spots and sensitive issues among our members.

But we began to make progress through a variety of educational components and action items. One of the most dramatic and influential elements of our strategy was dfree® Sunday. Every fourth Sunday of the month, we started pausing during worship to give parishioners the opportunity to share testimonials — bills they had paid on time, loans fulfilled, and credit cards paid off. At first, people were reluctant to tell their business in front of an entire church full of people. But when individuals experienced hundreds of people cheering after hearing their news of a student loan, car loan, or even mortgage paid in full, others began looking forward to giving their own testimonies. I'll never forget our celebration when one woman testified that she had finished paying off eleven credit cards!

You must remember that one of the primary ways of replacing the immediate gratification and compensation of using credit is to focus on your goal of financial freedom. This rather large abstract goal may not feel as satisfying as purchasing a new dress (or suit, in my case) or enjoying an exquisite meal in an upscale restaurant (that costs ten times the price of the ingredients). Which is all the more reason to make attaining your freedom a tangible reality through sharing and celebrating your successes with your support network or community. Celebrating with others helps them to hold you accountable to press on toward your ultimate goal. When you're struggling or feeling discouraged by how long the process may be taking, they can remind you of the successes they've seen you accomplish.

You're free to be as creative as you'd like in deciding how you want to celebrate. One member would host a potluck dinner every time she paid off a credit card. Others enjoyed taking their closest friends and supporters out for dessert or ice cream — as long as they stayed within budget. Some dfree® participants, once they reach a certain level of freedom from debt, like to host a children's Christmas party, fall harvest event, or Easter egg hunt. Which brings us to one of the most gratifying ways that dfree® participants seem to enjoy celebrating — giving back to other people.

Give

BACK

"Clearly, Pastor Soaries is on to something with the dfree® movement. I heard him speak at a training conference, and he challenged us in three areas: spiritually, intellectually, and economically.

"It astonished me how much sense he made as he used statistics to reveal the bad habits that we often refuse to admit. The whole time I'm sitting there thinking about how we can incorporate dfree® into our organization. I will recommend having Pastor Soaries come in and train a core leadership group. Then we hit it hard with putting on these type of no-nonsense training seminars around the communities.

"We can explain what it means to be a slave to debt and how we're weighed down by all those other bad financial habits we cling to, such as using those check cashing places, not having checking or savings accounts, carrying balances on multiple credit cards, not having life insurance, not monitoring our credit reports, and not making payments on time. The list goes on and on ... I see a vision here for a new way of life that can set so many people free to really live for the first time in their adult lives."

Thomas K., Camp Hill, PA

10

Invest in Others

Tithing, Leading, and Mentoring

RIGHT AFTER HURRICANE KATRINA, OUR CHURCH COLLECTED an offering that would be used to assist families devastated in the Gulf region. I was encouraged that we had collected a very healthy offering in one day and could offer direct assistance to dozens of families. After the service where we collected the special Katrina-designated offering, a well-dressed, highly educated young professional approached me and confessed that he wanted to give more to the Katrina Fund, but that he just did not have the money. This was shortly after we had started the dfree® ministry at the church.

His admission confirmed for me that knowledge and desire were insufficient for people who would really like to give back to others and help those in need. Many people sincerely want to give to worthy causes, their local church, or ministries that aid their community, but they simply cannot because they don't have it to give. They are missing out on a blessing and knowing the secret that giving to others helps us maintain the proper perspective on money as a gift from God, not an entitlement for ourselves.

After you've loosened the chains of financial slavery that have bound you for so long, and you've stabilized your debt and are experiencing ongoing success, then you're ready to make giving back a priority. Investing in others is one of the most life-giving, gratifying habits you can practice. In fact, one of the most life-changing, freeing actions you can take on your journey to being debt free is to make a regular financial contribution to your church or ministry organization.

As you may know, Christians usually refer to this as a tithe, a biblical term that simply means "tenth." My admonition to tithe each month may sound strange since in many areas I'm encouraging you to hold onto your money instead of allowing it to pass through your fingers like water. However, a commitment to the act of tithing produces divine dividends in our character and perspective that transcend financial matters. It allows us to stay focused on what truly matters most, forces us to acknowledge with gratitude what we do have, and contributes to God's kingdom in ways that save lives and redeem hearts.

Tithing often makes most of us uncomfortable, in part because we may not have an accurate understanding of all it entails. Many people ask me if they should give or how much they should give to the church or charities when they can't pay their credit card bills or mortgage. Obviously, you can only give what you have, not what belongs to someone else as it passes through your hands to them.

The Tithes That Bind

My own views on tithing have changed and led in part to my passion for dfree® living. Let me explain. When I first visited First Baptist Church as a pastoral candidate in 1990, I watched the interim pastor lead the congregation into the worship of giving. This is an act of worship. It is not intermission. It is not an extra time for the choir to perform, and it's not a break from the normal service. The giving of tithes and other offerings are expressions of honor and love and celebration of God just as much as any other element of the worship experience.

When the minister at First Baptist asked for the offering to begin, he asked all tithers to please stand. A smattering of people stood, and the minister directed them to walk to the front of the sanctuary to deposit their tithes in a special box that had been placed at the front of the pulpit.

I sat there and watched women with large hats and high heels clumsily climb over fragile elderly men, short round men with canes narrowly navigate their way through the long pews, and others employ a form of sanctified gymnastics as they pressed their way to the front of the church. Many seemed to be so proud to have this opportunity to prance around the church and put their generosity on display. As I watched this very uncomfortably, two thoughts entered my mind.

First, I thought about Jesus' admonition in Matthew 6:1–4 that we should give without public fanfare. "Be careful not to do your 'acts of righteousness' before men, to be seen by them. If you do, you will have no reward from your Father in heaven. So when you give to the needy, do not announce it with trumpets, as the hypocrites do in the synagogues and on the streets, to be honored by men. I tell you the truth, they have received their reward in full. But when you give to the needy, do not let your left hand know what your right hand is doing, so that your giving may be in secret. Then your Father, who sees what is done in secret, will reward you." This practice of tithers marching around the church seemed to violate the principle taught by Jesus.

My second thought was that if this church should select me as their pastor, the tithers' march was going to be the first change I would make as the pastor. On the first Sunday of November in 1990, I preached my first sermon as the third pastor of the First Baptist Church of Lincoln Gardens. Before it was time to deliver my sermon, I stood to lead the congregation in the worship of giving.

I began just as the interim pastor had begun by asking all tithers to stand. Once they had all stood, I invited them to join the rest of the congregation in taking a very good look at themselves and the others who were standing because this would be the last time they would ever be asked to stand during a service.

When challenged by some very influential people in the congregation who reminded me that I had not even been installed as pastor yet, I reminded them of the words of Jesus in Matthew 6. I also told them that many of the people who had been standing as tithers could not be giving anything close to 10 percent of their incomes based on the amount of their gifts, and that many others who probably were true tithers had never stood because they did not want the attention.

I understood early in my life that much of what we believe about adherence to the biblical admonitions on tithing is really more of a shallow show than what the prophet Malachi described in Malachi 3:10: "Bring the whole tithe into the storehouse." Tithing was not meant to be a parade or show-case. No, tithing was meant for the people of God to honor God with gratitude in a respectful and humble way.

Reciprocating God's Support

I have been tithing longer than I have been a Christian. My parents were strict tithers who were affiliated with a church where tithing was a core belief. In fact, the church of my youth would not allow a person to hold any official church position until they were certified by the church treasurer to be an "active, tithe-paying member."

The very word *tithe* means "one-tenth" of something. The act of tithing as we practice it in church means that we give one-tenth of what the Bible calls our "increase," or what we call our income, back to God, as Abraham gave to Melchize-dek in Genesis 14:17–20. And that was the initial basis of my concern about the practice of our church. How did the trea-surer know that members were really giving 10 percent of their income? Members were not asked to submit their income tax returns or their pay stubs to the treasurer (thank God!).

We did not know if members' tithing was based on their gross or net income. The treasurer could not determine if the individual had received a pay bonus or not. Suppose there had been garnishments on the wages of a member or deductions for savings, deferred compensation, or retirement investments. How would the church's treasurer really know who was a 10 percent giver?

But I must admit that having to tithe even before I really understood tithing has never hurt me. In fact, I believe that when I left the church and turned my back on God, the fact that I had been raised as a tither contributed significantly to my conscience about things that I had begun doing and my ultimate return to the Lord. This emerges from two key principles inherent in tithing:

1. God has blessed me so much that it is not unreasonable for me to give 10 percent of what God has enabled and blessed me to earn and possess back to God. In restaurants we are expected to give our waiter or waitress at least 15 percent of the cost of the meal just for serving the meal to us from the kitchen. Those of us who have received minimally satisfactory service from waiters or waitresses will understand my point: The waiter did not make the food or cook the food — God has certainly done more for me than any waiter at a restaurant. God deserves a tithe.

2. Tithing requires that I give to God first and make God my priority. It was an important part of my mental and spiritual development to be taught to think about God as soon as I received any money for anything. The point was not the money. The point was the recognition of my relationship with God.

When I said "any money for anything," I mean *anything*. If my tooth came out and the tooth fairy brought me a dollar, 10 cents went to God. If I received $25 for my birthday, $2.50 went in my tithe envelope. Although I resented this as a child, this actually instilled a sense of prioritizing God at a very young age. This is certainly one of the benefits of teaching and promoting tithing — especially among children.

The idea that God does trust us with all of what He blesses us to have and we then voluntarily bring 10 percent back to God and keep 90 percent is a very inspiring proposition. The federal government does not trust us the way God trusts us. The United States Treasury takes its money, our taxes, off the top, as it were, of our paychecks. If self-employed people fail to pay any taxes, the government will notice the failure and, one way or another, get tax payments from them. And if Uncle Sam takes more than he should, we have to chase him to get our refund with no interest. So I have never thought that tithing was too much for God to ask.

But this still does not resolve the issues of tithing accuracy and accountability. Our inability and appropriate unwillingness to probe more deeply into members' personal financial situations makes it impossible to establish whether or not anyone is actually tithing — or giving their 10 percent. The fact is that the identification of a tither is really a very subjective exercise that seems to detract from the spiritual principles that are supposed to be prominent in the practice.

Abraham did not give a tithe to Melchizedek in order to qualify for anything from humans or God. He blessed Melchizedek because of the blessing he had already received himself. In that sense, the very first actual tithe in the Bible was a not a "payment" — Abraham was not "paying" his tithes. He was giving a thanksgiving offering. Abraham was not making a conscious investment or consciously sowing a seed for the benefit of his own future. I say consciously because Abraham had already been tremendously blessed by God and obviously kept being blessed by God.

I believe that Abraham's blessings can be attributed to the fact that he demonstrated a willingness to be a blessing to others first. But Abraham's goal was not obtaining or having his blessings. In giving this tithe, Abraham was simply giving recognition to the source of his current blessings. In fact, after Abraham gave the tithe to Melchizedek, he refused to accept any of the king's gifts and would only pass these along to the men who had assisted Abraham. (See Genesis 14:18–24.)

No Quid Pro Quo

Unfortunately, many pastors, churches, and ministries have exploited the sacred act of tithing and created false and damaging expectations that when we give God our tithe as "seed money," He will then in turn bless us with a "harvest windfall." The stereotype of the slick, emotional televangelist who promises to pray for unseen, unidentified viewers in exchange for "gifts" to the ministry in specified amounts comes to mind. Basically, such exploitation reinforces the notion that God is our lottery genie, waiting to award us a jackpot that's ten times the amount of our tithing-ticket purchase.

This is one of my greatest concerns about tithing because it's such an inadequate, shallow understanding. We can become formulaic, expecting a quid pro quo relationship with God that flows from our tithe. We used to quote that Malachi text in church every week. We put special emphasis on the part of Malachi 3:8–12 that states:

> "Will a man rob God? Yet you rob me. But you ask, 'How do we rob you?' In tithes and offerings. You are under a curse — the whole nation of you — because you are robbing me. Bring the whole tithe into the storehouse, that there may be food in my house. Test me in this," says

the LORD Almighty, "and see if I will not throw open the floodgates of heaven and pour out so much blessing that you will not have room enough for it. I will prevent pests from devouring your crops, and the vines in your fields will not cast their fruit," says the LORD Almighty. "Then all the nations will call you blessed, for yours will be a delightful land," says the LORD Almighty.

This text is much more complicated than a simple guarantee that if we give God 10 percent, we will get more financial blessings than we can handle. It should not be a means of religious manipulation.

The passage ought to teach us — especially the religious leaders whom Malachi accused of stealing from God — that God wants to provide for us, but God also expects God's people to support God's work. For Malachi it was the Jerusalem temple built by Solomon and restored by Ezra and Nehemiah. For us it is God's church. We should not tithe to become blessed. We should tithe to support the God who supports us and have enough faith to know that God will supply for us.

What is often missed in the tithing message is that God does not divide our increase or our income, give us 90 percent and take His "cut" of 10 percent. No, *everything* we have belongs to God, and we give God at least 10 percent to give recognition and thanks to the God who owns it all. That is why asking people to tithe is not enough. We often say that we are giving God "what belongs to God." But if we did that, we would have to give God 100 percent.

When we give whatever we give to God, we are to give the best that we have, and 10 percent is a minimum that we should try to exceed. If our restaurant waiter is really good —

personable, attentive, helpful, knowledgeable, hospitable — we may actually leave a 20 or 25 percent tip. If we have a party of six or more, the restaurant will determine the amount of the gratuity on our bill and we pay it. Why should God deserve any less?

So tithing should not be approached legalistically or judgmentally. Tithing should not be seen as a proposition where God is turned into a cosmic Santa Claus, and we tithe to insure that our future requests are met. No, as my friend William Watley explains in *Bring the Full Tithe*, we should not tithe "because of what we expect in return but because we love God, and we love God enough to give our very best." Ultimately, tithing is a state of heart and mind.

The Art of Stewardship

Remember the parable of the talents that we noted at the end of chapter 4? You'll recall that at the conclusion of this parable, when the wealthy master returned to see how his three managers had fared, he praised the two who had invested wisely and made a profit, but he condemned the one who merely returned what he had been given.

Jesus also taught about trust and honesty in handling money. "Whoever can be trusted with very little can also be trusted with much, and whoever is dishonest with very little will also be dishonest with much. So if you have not been trustworthy in handling worldly wealth, who will trust you with true riches? And if you have not been trustworthy with someone else's property, who will give you property of your own?" (Luke 16:10–12).

First, we are really being given a perspective on the little that we have and how little we are asked to do with it. Our perspective on our earnings and our assets is an inappropriate perspective. To Jesus, whatever we have is very little, yet God has trusted us to manage it wisely and honestly. He even cautions us to understand that if we cannot handle the small stuff, then God will not be able to trust us with big stuff.

We often wonder why God has not blessed us with more of something. Jesus wants us to assess how well we have handled the business that we have. Perhaps God is waiting for us to prove ourselves trustworthy with the small stuff He has asked of us before He entrusts us with more. Jesus said that if we cannot handle worldly wealth, how can we be trusted with true riches? Have we wondered what those true riches are? Jesus is contrasting the things of this world with the things of the kingdom of God.

The fact that God has offered us ownership of a piece of God's kingdom may be incomprehensible to the average person. But a Christian is not an average person and can be expected to understand the benefit of true riches. The implications of this teaching by Jesus are life changing. This suggests that handling money, bills, and earthly financial matters is just practice for what God really wants us to handle. Suppose we really believed that. We would be less consumed with getting money to buy things and more focused on managing money to please and impress God. This is a radical change for most Christians, not to mention unbelievers. No wonder Paul said, "I have learned to be content whatever the circumstances" (Philippians 4:11).

Jesus concludes His wrap-up of the parable of the dishonest manager by asking about our handling of personal property. He wants to know who would trust someone to take care of their property who has not been able to handle their own business. Forget whether or not God will bless me with a new car if I "plant a seed in the ministry." God wants to give me a place in God's eternal kingdom and restore me to a position of dominion that was intended for me at Creation.

Tithing is just a small part of this program. God is looking for much more than tithers. God is looking for people who will love God with heart, soul, and mind. God is seeking those who will give cheerfully and not grudgingly. Jesus is looking for disciples who will deny themselves, take up their crosses, and follow Him. Tithing should be an active, organic part of your overall strategy to achieve debt-free living.

I compare tithing to the yeast that leavens the bread. When we give a tithe back to God, acknowledging with gratitude how He has blessed us with all that we do have, we practice the continual art of mindful stewardship. Our focus changes from an earthly perspective to an eternal viewpoint, releasing us from the hold that money and possessions would have over us and replacing that hold with godliness, generosity, and grace.

11

Ignite dfree® Living

dfree® Training,
Starting/Leading dfree® Movements

SHORT OF A MONASTIC LIFE, IT'S NEARLY IMPOSSIBLE TO LIVE in the modern world without spending money. While a cloistered life off the modern grid may sound appealing at times (particularly at the first of the month with a stack of unpaid bills before you), this is not a viable option or desirable solution for those enslaved by consumer debt. The exchange of some form of currency provides an economic and social foundation for almost everyone in the world.

Consequently, as we've seen throughout our analysis of our culture, we find ourselves pulled by a variety of social influences and cultural forces that sweep us off solid ground and into the rapids of credit, where we find ourselves drowning in debt. No matter how powerful or persuasive the culture of debt may be around us, however, we cannot blame our financial slavery on anyone but ourselves. As we begin to attain our financial freedom and gain a new perspective on what matters most in our lives, another primary way we give back is through sharing what we've learned from our own experiences.

As the larger culture becomes much more secular and in many ways more hostile to Christianity, churches face some very important decisions about their role in society. Do we give in to the culture and become mirror images of the greed, carnality, and materialism of the consumer culture? Do we become facilitators of the slavery of debt and, instead of prophesying against it, simply install ATM machines in our churches and set up merchant accounts that enable us to sell our products by accepting credit cards? Or do we attempt to impact the culture by preaching and teaching an alternative way to attain the abundant life that Jesus promised? What better way to make an impact on the culture than to reach the next generations?

Our youth represent the greatest evangelistic opportunity and challenge in the church. Young people are making critical decisions at much earlier ages than ever before. There was a time when Sunday school was sufficient to teach them using biblical stories, and then families nurtured them during the week to teach practical applications of the principles in those stories. Today children have unrestricted access to television, the Internet, satellite radio, cell telephones with text messaging, Facebook, Twitter, and only heaven knows what other new culture-changing media, all 24/7. They are bombarded with messages and images that infiltrate the privacy of our homes, and they have millions of options from which to choose for everything. But the openness also gives dfree® a viable strategic entry into the lives and preferences of children: dfree® addresses the subject of money.

Children have become a coveted market segment. As a

result, marketers have made children much more aware today than previous generations were about the need for money and the possible uses of money. What better population to teach biblical principles of money — saving, tithing, investing, giving, budgeting — and in so doing, show them that Jesus has plans for their lives and the way they live. One thing is certain: No child will ever get bored or distracted talking about money. And God can become more relevant than perhaps in any other way if God's plan for managing and using money is presented to our children before they become totally brainwashed by the consumer-driven culture.

Our entire nation is in deep trouble, and perhaps the largest indicator of our trouble is the level of our debt — not only family debt but national debt as well. The culture of debt that engulfs every level of government can erode the quality of life and the strength of the nation for generations. Even worse, when it comes to challenging certain countries on matters such as human rights, civil rights, women's rights, workers' rights, and religious freedom, we have become muzzled because some of the countries with the greatest repression, needs, and challenges are lending us money as we live above our means. The borrower is indeed slave to the lender!

The Power of Good News

More important than the financial gains have been the increases in institutional respect that dfree® has prompted. People generally want to believe in churches. The people who attend our churches want to be proud of the church they call their own. This pride should not be limited to esteem for their pastors. People should be able to boast to families, neighbors, and friends about the respect they have for the work their church is doing. The dfree® program creates that kind of affection for the church from within and without.

I went to meet a young man whose father had been arrested and needed to be bailed out of jail. This young man does not attend our church, but both of his parents do. When his father got into trouble, his mother called me, and I met the young man at the police station to help him arrange for his father's release. While we waited, the young man began describing his respect for our church and the things we do. He mentioned specifically our debt-free ministry that he said his mother always talked about. He understood it, he loved it, and, most important, he respected it.

Followers of Jesus should be a threat to injustice, unfairness, and ignorance. Unfortunately, too much of the scorn the church receives today emanates more from our arrogance, self-righteousness, and extravagance rather than our service, integrity, and morality. A movement such as dfree® that offers practical solutions to life-restricting problems can demonstrate that we are aware of our culture and its urgent needs.

As we make this change, we discover that our Father's loving restoration offers us much more than just membership in a local church. When evangelism becomes synonymous with church growth, then reaching people with the gospel is merely a membership drive for the church. Evangelism is the spread of the gospel and the gospel is truly good news — life-changing, destiny-altering good news. When we respond to God's free gift of unmerited grace, we are no longer limited by all the circumstances that seem to ensnare us. God made us for purposes much greater than living in the suburbs and drowning in debt.

Many dfree® participants are liberated by the good news that their family backgrounds do not determine their destinies. They can experience the joy of knowing God both here on earth as well as in heaven. I'm convinced that dfree® has the potential to be an evangelistic strategy precisely because it delivers good news about a matter that has entrapped people who have the potential to be set free from financial slavery.

Sevenfold Success

While it's not necessary to participate in a dfree® movement through a church or other ministry, doing so can certainly increase the likelihood of your success. From years of experience, I've identified seven factors that contribute to the success of our dfree® strategy in the local church. Even if you're not participating in a church-sponsored debt-free living program, I believe an awareness of these elements can inspire you in formulating your own unique strategy and personal plan.

1. Vision of the Leadership

There is no substitute for the vision of the leader in forming a successful strategy and then implementing its execution. For most churches, the leadership role is held by the senior pastor, whose vision must be accompanied by passion evident throughout the congregation. This vision cannot be delegated or assigned to a participant or someone outside the community. After all, it is the senior pastor whom people hear regularly; he or she inspires the church more than anyone else, and the people trust the senior pastor's authority more than that of anyone else at their church.

The element of trust may be the most important. We are

dealing with intensely emotional, deeply personal matters. Many church members would rather share their personal business with a stranger than with a member of the congregation where they have some modicum of respectability and status. The pastor must lead the way in assuring members of confidentiality with their financial business. The pastor is also the one who must challenge dfree® leaders and teachers to keep people's information strictly confidential.

In addition, the pastor must stay current with issues that relate to finance and debt. The people know the difference between the pastor truly having a vision for something and the pastor simply tolerating something that is someone else's vision. The best way for the pastor to communicate that vision is to live the vision. When we started dfree®, I had to commit to something personal and concrete to demonstrate a new level of devotion. As I shared earlier, by my willingness to go on a "necktie fast," I made it clear that everyone, including myself, always has room for growth and more financial discipline and accountability. Someone once told me that we cannot lead where we will not go ourselves. Member participation in dfree® activities depends on the vision and leadership of the leader of the flock.

The pastor must also use the pulpit to promote the idea of dfree®, the principles of dfree®, the activities of dfree®, and the rewards of dfree®. A dfree® church will have to hear sermons preached that awaken the congregation to the possibility of deliverance from the bondage of debt and the joy of living debt free. The pastor has more power than anyone else in the church or the community to motivate people toward financial freedom.

2. Buy-In of Other Leaders

Every leader needs a team to be effective, and a senior pastor is no different. Although the senior pastor is key to the success of dfree®, the buy-in, consensus, support, and participation of the leadership of the church is also important. When I first arrived at First Baptist Church, someone asked me at a church business meeting if I had a vision for the church. I told her that I did have a vision for the church. She waited, and when she realized that this was all I had planned to say, she asked me to share with the members what my vision was. I answered by telling her that I was not going to tell her. I went on to add that I would not tell the church members my vision for the church until the church members told me their vision for the church. After we developed a shared vision for the church — mine and theirs — then we would be prepared to go forward.

While the senior pastor may be the most influential person in the church, it is not true that the senior pastor is the most influential person in every individual member's life on every matter. There are informal "pastors" throughout the church who have tremendous influence among many of the members. Therefore, these leaders must be allowed to "catch the vision" of the pastor and reinforce what people hear from the pulpit in various settings. We don't want one message coming from the pastor and then a different message being sent by the "sub-pastors" throughout the congregation. The elders, deacons, deaconesses, stewards, ministers, presidents, coordinators, leaders, trustees, auxiliary heads, missionaries, and other heads of units within the church need to be in one accord on this undertaking.

3. Formal Leadership Training

The leaders cannot share the vision unless they receive formal dfree® training. They have to know what dfree® is, why the pastor is bringing the strategy to the church, the benefits for the church, and the benefits for the leaders. In most instances we don't spend enough time equipping, nurturing, and assisting our church's leaders.

I have found that some of the people leading ministries in our churches are the people who are hurting the most. They give their time, they spend time away from their families, they volunteer their services, they are held to high standards of accountability — and then they are often overlooked as people who also really need the help and support of the church. The dfree® leadership training should not be offered simply as training or with the impression of what-else-does-the-church-want-them-to-do-as-service. The dfree® leadership training should be offered as a benefit for leaders. It gives leaders a chance to preview what church members will receive. And if needed, it will help them deal with their own financial challenges.

We found that some of our leaders were losing their homes or considering bankruptcy; some were victims of identity theft, were unemployed, or were part of families facing eviction. Our leaders needed help writing wills, identifying appropriate insurances, making investment decisions, developing family budgets, and everything else covered in the four dfree® levels. When leaders enjoy the benefits of dfree®, it becomes easier for them to help support and promote the vision among the members.

4. Structured Membership Education

Success in dfree® includes having ongoing structured education for members. This may mean making dfree® classes a part of the church's regular educational program. We launched dfree® at First Baptist Church by having every Sunday school class and every Bible study class use materials that taught God's plan concerning finances. The dfree® education component will also include offering specific classes that cover the range of topics on introductory and more advanced levels.

The fact that all levels of topics are covered destigmatizes dfree® and makes it relevant for people in every economic category. The dfree® program is as much for people who are millionaires as it is for the unemployed. The classes must all begin on time, end on time, and follow the curriculum being used. Classes should be scheduled to make it convenient for members to attend. Only qualified people should be allowed to teach the content.

5. Creation of a Movement

At a dfree® committee meeting I asked this question: "Why did Barack Obama defeat Hillary Clinton in the 2008 Democratic presidential primary elections?" No one was able to answer the question correctly. Mrs. Clinton was favored to win — she had more qualified staff, more political experience, started with more big-name endorsements, and had higher polling numbers when she started than Mr. Obama. How, then, did a freshman senator with a controversial name become the first African American nominee and later President of the United States, defeating a former First Lady and a former war hero?

The answer: Mrs. Clinton and then Mr. McCain ran campaigns. Mr. Obama created a movement.

Although there are some effective elements associated with a campaign, I use the word *movement* here because a movement goes beyond a campaign by reaching the emotional regions of the human personality. Rather than being a program for a few, a dfree® movement impacts the entire congregation and its culture. The dfree® program ought to feel like a movement and function like a movement utilizing some of the elements of an effective campaign. We must make it socially popular to eliminate bills, save money, and get out of debt. That means, for instance, that dfree® announcements require more than a two-line mention in the church bulletin. As the young people would say, dfree® has to go on "full blast."

Like a campaign, dfree® needs banners, posters, and other forms of promotional materials placed in strategic locations around the church. The dfree® pledge cards also help to promote the campaign. The point is to promote dfree® the same way we would promote our favorite candidate for mayor of our city. No one should be asking, "What is dfree®?" at First Baptist Church anymore. They may not be dfree® yet, but they certainly know what dfree® is.

6. Ongoing Visibility

The dfree® program can start with people setting debt reduction goals and joining the Billion Dollar Challenge (BDC). The BDC is a dfree® web-based movement for individuals and groups to set, track, and celebrate debt reduction progress (www.billiondollarpaydown.com). The goal is to help people pay off one billion dollars of debt!

In keeping with the movement theme, dfree™ requires ongoing visibility in the church. People have grown used to our special emphases, special themes, special days, and special projects. Features like these usually spell "short-term," and it is generally not long before we move on to the next something rather quickly. But if we are really serious about helping our people out of the bondage of debt, we must be prepared for a long-term ministry. First Baptist Church started this ministry in 2005, and I feel like we are just scratching the surface. To keep the movement moving and to get maximum participation, dfree® must maintain maximum visibility in the life of the church. In time, "special" ought to signal "normal" in people's minds when they think of dfree®.

In addition to the banners and posters that can be prominently displayed, dfree™ can remain visible by means of the following:

- Special dfree® events covering particular financial topics
- dfree® promotions and competitions
- dfree® skits and creative productions
- dfree® field trips to educational and motivational venues

The point is to offer variety and continuity in order to provide visibility for the dfree® movement.

7. Celebrations

The first time I attended a preschool graduation, I thought it was preposterous. This was because I did not have a child in preschool. Nor was I a graduating preschool student. What made little sense to me was a huge event in the lives of those involved.

It can be a big accomplishment to pay off one credit card if the person never dreamed that it was possible to pay it off. It can be a liberating moment to see the title to a car that finally belongs to you. I have seen people shed tears when announcing that they actually finished paying their student loans. These feelings should be recognized and punctuated by celebrations. This can encourage that person and others to take the next step.

How you structure your blueprint for financial freedom is up to you and should be custom crafted for your particular situation. I encourage you, if at all possible, to form your own dfree® group if you aren't already part of a church or other community committed to debt-free living. An effective strategy plan should include a list of individuals who know you're committed to dfree® living. These should be people you can trust with your situation who are willing to listen, encourage, and motivate you to achieve your goals.

Finally, an effective strategy must celebrate each milestone, each debt paid in full, each payment made on time, each purchase made with cash. If you incorporate these major components into your strategy for debt-free living, you will have a key that unlocks your financial future. Better yet, you'll be part of a movement that can change the world.

12

Impact the Culture

Setting Examples,
Pointing Others to Freedom

AS WE'VE SEEN, THERE'S NO MISSION MORE CENTRAL TO THE current needs of the American people than that of helping to relieve the pressures of financial oppression. From the many diverse participants of dfree®, we've experienced consistent success in virtually every economic category. I'm convinced that our success emerges from the fact that dfree® is not only a rescue program for the financially distressed but a comprehensive motivational strategy to help people develop a new lifestyle relative to their deepest longings — longings that cannot be satisfied by the love of money or the idolatry of what money can buy, but only through the love of God as experienced in an ongoing, day-to-day, eternal relationship.

The dfree® program and its participants create opportunities for a lasting, culture-changing impact in people's lives. They provide what the church often refers to as an evangelistic outreach and expand the church's capacity to create new relationships with people outside of the church. We have found that people who will not visit the church on a Sunday morning will attend a dfree® class on a Tuesday or Thursday night. The need for help in this area is so pervasive that people will accept help from almost anywhere. And that really should be another motivation for the church. Financial pressure leads to desperation, and desperation can make people quite vulnerable to scams that make their problems worse.

High numbers of families that came to us for assistance to avoid foreclosures on their homes had already been victims of illegitimate businesses that took advantage of their situations and ripped them off. This is an urgent issue for our elderly members and neighbors. There are financial vultures who prey on our seniors, and churches must help them avoid making terrible mistakes. It is easier to do this within the context of a ministry like dfree®. We have also conducted classes in Spanish for the growing Hispanic population near our church.

The common factor that unites all groups today is the need to improve our financial lives. But we would have never been able to connect with these families had we limited our outreach to invitations during Sunday morning worship or alongside requests to attend Bible study.

The dfree® program offers an opportunity to take the church beyond the four walls of the building. Because of its secular appeal and outcomes, dfree® is easily adaptable to any audience and environment. The information being provided by the church helps the church bridge whatever gaps exist between itself and its community. And even when a church or group uses a curriculum that does not include a faith component, like the very good government-created "Money Smart," a comprehensive financial education curriculum designed to help individuals outside the financial mainstream enhance their financial skills, a Christian presenter will be able to affirm the gospel as he or she presents it. It is still evangelism even if Jesus, God, and the Bible are never mentioned.

The gospel can often be understood better when people *see* the love of Jesus rather than simply *hear* about the love of Jesus. That means that dfree® can and should be offered in beauty shops, libraries, schools, pizza shops, firehouses, and in homes — anywhere the church can meet with people and serve their needs. We have started dfree® classes in the barbershop across the street from our church and are offering it to public housing residents in the community room where they live. Many participants would have never come inside the church even on a Tuesday night. When we meet them where they are, through us they get a chance to see Jesus as He is.

The results of strategic outreach can be phenomenal. There are many churches that do an effective job going door-to-door, sharing the gospel message with people and praying for people's needs with them in their homes. I was at a church in California where leaders were training members to meet people at bus stops and train stations and invite them to church to talk with them about Jesus. This effort was amazing, and the pastor later told me it yielded great results for the church. Such work is always appropriate when it can be effective.

However, in certain areas of the country, we are unlikely to attract many people to visit homes or even share the gospel with people on street corners. Moreover, there are people in our churches who would not engage in that type of ministry even if they thought that Jesus Himself would appear and lead the team. We have found that some of these very people who would never do outreach or "missionary work" are eager to be a part of the dfree® ministry. I call them our financial missionaries. They are people on a mission to serve the financial needs of others in the name of Jesus.

It is unfortunate to have people in the pews of the church who are not attracted to traditional ministries and feel these ministries have nothing that matches their interests or skills. The dfree® program has given us a way to involve many of those people, and they serve with enthusiasm. This is one of the tangible outcomes — real evangelism actually strengthens the church.

The most impactful evangelist of the twentieth century was Billy Graham. When Mr. Graham conducted a crusade in a particular city, the churches in that city prepared for two to three years in advance of the event. They had Bible studies, conducted prayer meetings, and trained counselors to serve new converts — all in advance of the crusade. Many pastors participated in the Graham crusade, but not because they thought Mr. Graham was a great preacher or because they wanted good seats for themselves in the stadium when he arrived. Many pastors participated because they knew that their churches could become better churches as a result of the preparatory process and the work that would occur after Billy Graham left. We learned that in our Paterson New Jersey Youth Crusades. Churches that had no clue on how to attract and engage more young people became much more youth friendly as a result of participating in the Youth Crusade process. Likewise, churches that get involved with dfree® will find that their church becomes a stronger church with more participation from members who otherwise would be solely "pew members."

Is the Caller There?

We need a culture change that makes practical ministries such as dfree® normal, expected behaviors of those of us who follow Jesus. Unfortunately, we often maintain a very limiting view of how the church can provide resources, community support, and ongoing encouragement. I will never forget a radio interview that I did for a Milwaukee, Wisconsin, radio station. A local radio personality had seen me on a national television program, and he invited me to be interviewed by telephone on his show. After we discussed some of my views on various issues, and I shared with him information about some of the initiatives sponsored by the church I serve, he invited his listeners to call his program to ask me questions.

The second caller expressed enthusiastic support for all of the ideas and concepts I had mentioned. He was very complimentary and encouraged other listeners to consider my words as being quite valuable. But the caller also had a serious concern. He expressed confusion about why a clergyperson, a Baptist minister, would be the one discussing issues like education, economics, crime, housing, and political representation. His view was that I was saying the right things, but I was the wrong person to be saying them. After all, he asserted, that is not the role of a minister. By implication he seemed to also suggest that the topics we were discussing were not within the proper scope of a church's role.

His statement reminded me of a comment someone else made to me. This person said that I would be a better minister if I were not so busy trying to help the community. Both of these individuals expressed a common view that many people possess about the role of Christian clergy and Christian churches. Having been reminded that this perspective does exist, I realized there could even be those who read this book and honestly see no relationship between my primary vocation of Christian minister, the responsibilities of the Christian church, and the issue of financial literacy and economic self-sufficiency. Perhaps it would make more sense to many if my book were a commentary on the Bible or a discussion about matters religious. What may be disconcerting for some people is that I don't believe in just "sticking to religion," as some people say it.

Of course, an easy way to avoid criticism and explain the dfree® project would be to simply state that writing is an extracurricular pursuit for me, and that I am best understood to be bivocational — a minister and a writer — as if this work is actually a secondary activity. There are those who would probably readily accept the explanation that I write books, articles, and newspaper columns about social issues as a personal pastime or a hobby I enjoy when I take off my proverbial clerical collar. Of course, I do not actually wear a clerical collar. The point is that some people would probably understand and accept that explanation.

The truth is that writing and speaking about social issues like family finances and personal debt and working on projects that help families address their daily financial challenges are not departures from my role of minister. Rather, they are central to my understanding of Christian ministry and the role of the church. So my hope, through the dfree® movement, is to offer a vision for the church's role in promoting economic freedom for the millions of Americans who are victims of the economy rather than participants in its recovery.

Jesus made it clear that He had been called and sent into

a ministry of deliverance, salvation, and liberation. As an adult, He returned to His hometown, Nazareth, and went to the synagogue to participate in the Sabbath activities. Luke 4:18–19 says that Jesus stood and read a passage from the prophet Isaiah: "The Spirit of the Lord is on me, because he has anointed me to preach good news to the poor. He has sent me to proclaim freedom for the prisoners and recovery of sight for the blind, to release the oppressed, to proclaim the year of the Lord's favor."

The financial state of many church attendees and people who live in neighborhoods surrounding churches qualifies them to be described as poor, prisoners, blind, and oppressed. We may wear our Sunday best and smile at those sitting on the pew next to us, but beneath this pleasant veneer we find individuals struggling to survive, overwhelmed by the desperation caused by their finances.

It is not productive to marginalize the Word in a way that requires making distinctions between the physical and spiritual aspects of these words Christ read from Isaiah. Today we make false distinctions between physical and spiritual poverty, physical and spiritual captivity, and physical and spiritual deliverance. Such distinctions cause some people to believe that Jesus was only interested in saving souls, or that He was solely focused on political and social justice. This divide has been a source of tension for evangelicals and mainline churches in America for over a century.

But neither Isaiah nor Jesus made such distinctions. It is inconceivable that physical bondage and pain would have no impact on one's spiritual state and vice versa. It is also absurd to assume that Jesus would be committed to reaching the human soul while ignoring the body in which that soul resides. What is clear is that spiritual poverty contributes to and exacerbates one's economic poverty — and one's economic deprivation can undermine one's spiritual vitality.

Keep the Change

If all we do is demonize debt, then those who find themselves in trouble may just go undercover and keep their problems to themselves. We need others to affirm the changes they are trying to make. While I believe the church is uniquely qualified to offer this kind of support, it's certainly not the only safety net available. However, the church is uniquely poised to influence cultural values by meeting people where they're living, by addressing their biggest struggles and most challenging circumstances.

In her very important book *The Overspent American*, Professor Juliet B. Schor of Boston University states, "Frugality could become a socially acceptable consideration." She recommends that people attempting to break the cycle of borrowing and spending and who want to defy the culture of "more is better" should find a "reference group" that subscribes to the new culture. Again, since I have witnessed incredible success inside the church, I know that it can offer this kind of counter-cultural community.

However, the church itself holds no special power or privilege to eliminate your debt and transform your life. Only you can make that change and escape financial slavery through the power of God. In fact, the main reason I believe we can change the culture is because we have access to the power of God. Since He cares about us and is committed to delivering us from evil, then the battle is not ours — it belongs to God.

12. *Impact the Culture*

While Hollywood, Madison Avenue, and other centers of media and entertainment power effectively entice us with seductive marketing, they do not have the ultimate source of power: the love of God and the transformational power of the gospel. They may have money, technology, and human talent, but they cannot draw on the supernatural strength of the Creator of the universe like we can.

Too often we look at our culture and cave in without even a fight, as if we have no other choices, alternatives, or resources than those dictated by the culture at large. When we put our minds to it, set our actions in motion, and invest our complete faith in God, we can do more than resist the power of culture over us. We can *change* the culture. Keeping up with the Joneses can be a good thing if the Joneses are living within their means, paying their bills on time, and saving money to maintain their hard-won freedom.

My hope and prayer for you is that you experience not only the unfettered freedom of being debt free but the exuberant joy that comes from freedom in Christ. May God bless your endeavors as you break the shackles of financial slavery and discover more of the person He created you to be. My only request is that if the dfree® principles help you that you invest what you've learned in the people around you, with the goal of revealing the love of our Father, who sent His only Son as a sacrifice so that all of us held captive by any stronghold or dark power may at last be truly free.

For Leaders Launching the dfree® Movement

FOR SEVERAL YEARS I TRAVELED FULLTIME AS A YOUTH SPEAKER, and each week found myself in a different city for an event. As soon as I arrived at the location for a given week, I could quickly tell whether I would participate in a successful event. The person picking me up at the airport would reveal my first clue. If the event leader was the one waiting to meet me, I began to worry. This usually indicated that the leader had taken on too much responsibility and was trying to handle the entire program personally. If a volunteer or hospitality coordinator met me, I became optimistic that the chief planner or event leader knew how to delegate effectively and make the most of the event team.

The key lesson to learn here for launching dfree® is this: you cannot do it alone. No one person can ignite dfree® on the scale needed to facilitate its ongoing success without a core group of people committed to the vision. The temptation is that an individual encounters dfree®, experiences great advancements toward his or her financial freedom, and then attempts to start a dfree® movement in his or her civic group, professional organization, or church. Without the vision, support, delegation, and implementation of a team, one person simply cannot tackle all the details needed to ensure success.

People who find themselves in leadership often tend to

think that their authority alone will be enough to launch dfree®. This mindset is a particular hazard for pastors. With so many different details to attend to within the church, almost everyone expects the pastor — usually the most visible, full-time paid employee of the church or ministry — to handle everything and anything. Such an expectation reveals the paradox most leaders, including pastors, experience. On the one hand, no one has the responsibility, influence, or authority like the pastor or leader. Nothing significant can really happen without at least having the pastor's blessing or the leader's approval. On the other hand, if the pastor tries to do everything himself or the leader allows herself to be the only resource for implementing change, even a very small church or group's undertaking will suffer significantly.

In order to launch dfree® successfully, a pastor or leader cannot simply be a great preacher or teacher. Nor is a passion to see his or her members become dfree® — no debts, no delinquencies, no deficits — enough to ignite action. The leader must also have a passion for organizing a team committed to dfree® education and implementation.

Teach from Experience

In virtually every field, whether academic or professional, the best educators teach from their own experiences. Informing others about dfree® living is no exception, and it's crucial that dfree® team members practice what they preach. However, I realize that when launching dfree® in a new setting, it may be necessary or even likely that many team members will find dfree® concepts new to them. One of my primary motives in writing this book is the hope that it can be used as a primer on debt-free living for those individuals longing to be set free from financial slavery. Team members should have read, digested, and discussed the material in these pages with the leader, and among themselves, prior to launching a movement within their church or organization.

While I pray that this book will be helpful in equipping team members, I realize that a quick overview of dfree® assumptions, core principles, and four levels of participation may be helpful in a variety of ways. So allow me to distill these for you here. While this information may be a matter of review for you if you've already read the book, it can also serve as a 50,000-foot aerial view that introduces a comprehensive picture of the heart of dfree®.

dfree® Core Assumptions

The dfree® strategy is built upon several key strategic assumptions:

1. dfree® invites people to learn and celebrate in group settings in addition to one-on-one counseling sessions. People are more likely to be successful at changing their economic lifestyles by participating with other people than they would alone.

2. dfree® is designed to guide a variety of diverse people at every financial level, thereby removing the stigma attached to a "crisis intervention" or "failure recovery" program intended only for people experiencing immediate distress. There are just as many upper middle-income families that have inadequate insurance

as there are low-income families without bank accounts. By having four different levels of teaching objectives, dfree® is inclusive of everyone, from people receiving Section 8 rental vouchers to people owning millions of dollars' worth of real estate. dfree® is not credit repair — it is a lifestyle upgrade and expansion.

3. dfree® uses campaign-like events and merchandise to create an atmosphere of enthusiasm and encouragement as often as possible. Every group gathering (including Sunday morning worship for churches) is an opportunity to celebrate dfree® successes and dfree® service.

4. dfree® is a process that takes time. Therefore, dfree® invites people to set goals that take a reasonable amount of time to accomplish and must be considered an ongoing lifestyle commitment, not a quick fix.

5. dfree® celebrates small victories to help keep people motivated to continue in the process. When we struggle together with others, we must also celebrate and enjoy the victories together.

6. dfree® has its own curriculum, "dfree® Lifestyle: 12 Steps to Financial Freedom." The national dfree® staff offers free training to churches, organizations, and individuals that are implementing dfree®. The dfree® website www.mydfree.org links to many resources that can be used in conjunction with a dfree® initiative.

7. dfree® is a ministry and/or community service that assumes no fee will ever be charged for a dfree® activity or class.

Key Tactics of dfree® Strategy

There are four key elements in the dfree® strategy: the word dfree®, the dfree® logo, the dfree® pledge card, and dfree® tools.

1. The word "dfree®"

This word places the emphasis on freedom from debt, delinquencies, and deficits, and on freedom to make Deposits in bank accounts, earn Dividends from investments, and own assets that have Deeds. By limiting the mention of the problems to one letter "d", it uses language psychologically to subordinate and suppress their power and influence. When a person says that they are trying to be dfree®, the words *debt, delinquencies,* and *deficits* have been relegated to the backseat without giving them any mention at all. It sounds positive even before someone knows exactly what it means. It is nonthreatening and does not subject someone to an implicit admission of problems as the term "debt free" may do. We created the word and now own the word (thus, the registered symbol®), protecting it from ever being used in a manner that differs from our intent.

2. The dfree® logo

This image is a contemporary interpretation of a carving I received as a gift from a church in Ghana. The carving depicts a man helping a younger man into a tree that the young man is attempting to climb, boosting him up with outstretched arms. The dfree® logo represents someone who is financially solvent — in economic terms "in the black" — boosting someone else toward financial freedom — being in the green (represented as grey in this book).

3. The dfree® pledge card

This plastic card that looks and feels like a credit card has proven to be an effective way to promote dfree®, maintain a commitment to being dfree®, and is also used as a tool to recruit people to become dfree®. The pledge card is tailored to belong to the sponsoring church or organization by placing specific information about the dfree® sponsor right on the card — photo, phone number, website, etc. We urge people to put the card near their credit cards to remind them not to use them to go into debt. This is our dfree® pledge card.

Front of pledge card

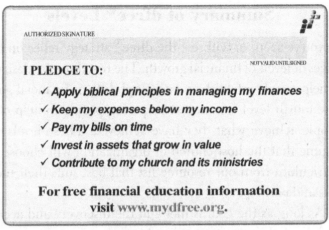

Back of pledge card

4. dfree® tools

dfree® creates proprietary tools and merchandise that dfree® participants can use to aid their efforts to live the dfree® lifestyle.

The official dfree® website's URL is www.mydfree.org. This site functions as a resource for individuals, organizations, and churches that are committed to participating in the dfree® movement.

Summary of dfree® Levels

As you've seen, or will see, the dfree® strategy relies on four stages or levels of financial growth. The first three are designed to help people establish and accomplish their financial goals. The fourth level is aimed at preparing people to help other people achieve what they have achieved. These levels also assume that the host church or organization will choose the curriculum from our resource list that best suits their members and participants.

As long as the goal is met and the discovery and accomplishment objectives are realized, any sound curriculum may be used successfully. The most important aspect of this work is that the strategy keeps people motivated, affirmed, and excited while they are using the curriculum of choice. Each dfree® level has specific learning and experiential objectives.

Level I — Get Started

This level is for the person who needs what I needed when I first started listening to that radio program about financial matters. This is for beginners.

Goal: To introduce the participant to the basic aspects of managing life and handling money

Discovery: The participant gains a clear understanding of his or her current financial status.

Accomplishments:

- Establish life goals
- Track spending
- List income and bills

- Establish banking relationship
- Secure all financial documents and records

Recommended reading of key resource: Jerrold Mundis, *How to Get Out of Debt, Stay Out of Debt and Live Prosperously* (New York: Bantam, 1988)

Level II — Get Control

This level is for people who have a little knowledge about personal finance, but who have not begun to implement a financial plan.

Goal: To actually begin the process of financial improvement

Discovery: The participant increases finance-related vocabulary and gains an understanding of real estate.

Accomplishments:

- Create spending plan
- Start Power Savings
- Start making Power Payments
- Set retirement goals

Recommended reading of key resource: Robert T. Kiyosaki, *Rich Dad, Poor Dad* (Paradise Valley, AZ: TechPress, 1998)

Level III — Get Ahead

This level is for people who have their basic financial house in order but need to protect their assets, make investment decisions, and enhance their long-term strategies.

Goal: To complete a total financial plan and prepare the participant for financial self-sufficiency

Discovery: The participant explores basic aspects of the stock market and considers investment options and actions.

Accomplishments:

- Save more money
- Buy insurance
- Estate planning/create or update wills
- Increase personal income
- Plan for retirement

Recommended reading of key resource: Ramit Sethi, *I Will Teach You to Be Rich* (New York: Workman Publishing, 2009)

Level IV — Give Back

This level is for people who are dfree® and are prepared to learn how to help others become dfree®. Some might call this "train the dfree® trainer."

Goal: To teach people to become dfree® leaders and instructors

Discovery: The participant gains confidence and can communicate, using an expanded financial vocabulary.

Accomplishments:

- Maintained credit score
- Built wealth
- Completed dfree® trainer training
- Created plan to give 14 volunteer hours to dfree® work
- Identified place to serve

Recommended reading of key resource: Juliet B. Schor, *The Overspent American: Why We Want What We Don't Need* (New York: Basic Books, 1998)

Organization in Action

Every great leader needs an even greater team if the vision is to come to fruition. Organization is the key to any success, and dfree® is no different. In order to infiltrate the culture of debt in a congregation or community, the pastor or leader must identify people who will be as committed to working for this cause as passionately as he or she believes in it. Depending on the personality of the group, this may be a bit more challenging than forming a traditional ministry of the church or task force within an organization.

Challenges of Forming a dfree® Committee

The first challenge is that this is a new focus, and people are not familiar with what will be expected. When someone signs up for the ushers' ministry or the scholarship committee, the mission and the tasks are clear. Unless a church or organization has a pre-existing economic empowerment or financial education committee or ministry, a special ministry like dfree® may have no history in the church or organization and therefore may be unknown to the members. It is hard to ask people to sign up for something that is completely unknown.

The second challenge is that the ministry's focus is so specific that people often think that only experts in the subject of finance are eligible for the committee. While it is true that certain activities in dfree® require some financial expertise, remember that this is a campaign — actually, a movement — that has many roles for people with skills unrelated to the field of finance. Just like civil rights activists did not have to be experts in civil rights laws to be effective, dfree® volunteers do not all have to be experts on financial management or debt relief strategies to make a meaningful contribution to the cause.

A possible third challenge relates to resistance to the ministry among the members at large — especially in the early stages — which can be intimidating and discouraging for those inclined to help. It can be unpopular to work on a ministry that asks people to reveal their financial weaknesses and get help with their challenges. In fact, many church members do not want anyone else in the church to "know their business" and would rather go to someone outside the church for assistance.

When we started the mortgage assistance portion of the dfree® ministry at First Baptist, we guaranteed our members that no member of the church would have access to their information. We used a third party mortgage-banking firm to analyze and process information our members submitted. We actually required the staff from that firm to sign confidentiality statements, committing themselves to the highest principles of integrity, honesty, and secrecy. Still, many members have been a bit squeamish about participation in the initiative — and that is putting it mildly.

The final and perhaps most daunting challenge is that so many people need dfree® themselves, it is hard to convince people that they can work as a dfree® leader even while struggling with financial issues themselves. I learned this when I selected our first dfree® chairman at First Baptist Church in 2005. I recruited someone who had great organizational and outstanding communications skills and was a successful professional in the financial industry. His effectiveness as a dfree® leader, however, had less to do with any of those attributes and everything to do with the fact that early in the process, he disclosed publicly — to the whole church — that although he was the congregation's dfree® leader, he needed dfree® himself and looked forward to becoming dfree®. Wow!

The dfree® chairman's transparency gave hundreds of members permission to participate in what the ministry had prepared for them. As we attempt to help our people overcome the burden of debt and enter the freedom of debt-free living, we are all what author Henri Nouwen would call "wounded healers." But it can be tough recruiting people who do not want to seem hypocritical about struggles they continue to have themselves.

Notwithstanding the challenges of recruiting leaders, a committed and dedicated group of people must have dfree® as their priority every day and every time they walk into the church. Our church has volunteer nurses and health care professionals who see the entire church operation from the perspective of health care and treatment of health-related emergencies. Our security ministry does the same thing from a security perspective. Our trustees want to know how much an activity or an item costs. This is the kind of intense focus that is needed from a dfree® committee. Every time the church meets, every time a ministry in the church gets together, everything that the church communicates should be seen by dfree® committee members as another opportunity to spread the message, sign up students for classes, or promote a special dfree® event to the congregation.

Preparing to Form a Team

Before identifying the types of people who will serve in this ministry, remember these seven important principles about the formation of a committee for dfree®.

1. *Take time to pray about your choices.* Pastors and leaders are exposed to so much pressure and subject to so much stress that we have a tendency to grab the first hand and every hand that offers to help. The issue of financial problems is so sensitive, though, that we cannot be too careful in choosing the people who lead its ministry. In many ways the first deacons selected in Acts 6 were called to a ministry that responded to financial needs within the congregation. The women of Greek descent felt that they were not receiving treatment equal to the women of Jewish descent, and they asked the disciples for help (6:1). Perhaps the matter needed adjudication because of cultural or even racial attitudes. But the underlying issue was that there were people with financial needs among the early Christians. Had the need not existed, there may not have been this sort of role for the deacons at all. The criteria were precise. The disciples wanted men "full of the Spirit" who were respected among the people they would be serving (6:3). These are the same kind of qualities that people need who will be helping others with their debts, their bills, and their financial lives.

To be sure, the committee members will not all be providing financial advice. And they certainly do not have to be ordained as deacons for this ministry. But the entire ministry team must have the personality and character of the first deacons in the Jerusalem church. The initial credibility of the ministry will match the credibility of the pastor and dfree®

committee members. The church will take dfree® as seriously as they take these leaders. Therefore, before selecting dfree® leaders for the church, one must be prayerful, asking God to both reveal and connect the right people for this important ministry. It is better to move slowly and choose the right people than to move quickly and regret the people appointed to lead. And those selected need time to consider the invitation, speak with their spouses, and pray about the work themselves before making a commitment to serve.

2. Ask people to serve for a specific period of time. Many people avoid getting involved in church ministry because they are not prepared to commit to service for the rest of their lives. There is always someone in the church who has held their position since Abraham left his hometown, and that is commendable and admirable. But every time we congratulate and thank a wonderful church worker for their decades of service, someone else is sitting in a pew, telling themselves it is inconceivable to even think about doing something for that length of time.

The key to recruiting people for ministry assignments today is to be specific about the length of time they are being asked to serve. I never ask anyone to serve for more than one year. In some cases the request is for six months. It is always better to extend someone's time commitment than it is to have them withdraw because they fear getting stuck in a position.

3. Clearly describe what you are asking people to do. When we were preparing to open our church bookstore, the staff complained there were no responses to our requests for volunteers. When I looked at the announcement, I noticed that it simply said the bookstore was opening soon and that we needed volunteers to work in it. Like those who don't want to work forever, most people don't respond well to open-ended requests to help out. I asked the staff how many hours the average volunteer would work per week, they told me three to five hours per week. The next Sunday, the announcement asked for volunteers who would give three to five hours a week. That Sunday they received all the responses they needed. Recruiting dfree® volunteers works the same way.

The more specific we can be about the number of hours per week, the frequency and length of meetings, the goals of the committee, the tasks that need to be performed, and other details related to the assignment, the easier it will be to attract good people to the ministry. Good people will give time as long as their time is not being wasted.

4. Choose people who can work with other people. A lot of talented people cannot work with other people. All dfree® leaders must be people people. Almost every task they will perform will be done alongside other people. Also, every leader may have to perform functions in addition to the planned tasks. For instance, at any given time a volunteer may have to stand in for a class leader who had an emergency, or register someone for an event. The one quality that all dfree® leaders must have is an outgoing personality that meshes well with other people. Being able to work with others means:

- Being flexible and open to change

- Able to adapt easily to new circumstances

- Able to avoid arguments to prove that their position is correct

- Tolerant and accepting of different points of view

- Able to delegate tasks to others

- Able to communicate instructions calmly

- Willing to work with people beyond their normal circle of friends

- Disinterested in personal recognition

- Open to constructive criticism and helpful suggestions

- Able to work for the greater good

- Able to keep the cause in the focus of all work

- Able to serve and not be served

5. *Avoid people who have products or services they want to sell.* The first people to volunteer and offer to help with dfree® will predictably be people who have either services or products to sell. As tempting as it is to let them join the committee, we cannot turn our ministry over to people whose interest is primarily sales. This is difficult to do because these people are trained to be strategic in their approaches to "help." Most of them are good people who sell insurance, financial services, investment funds, legal services, accounting services, tax advice, and even debt reduction services. This can be hard to manage because often the members of the church with the most expertise are the very ones we cannot allow to have direct, ongoing contact with members. The church cannot appear to give preferential treatment to any particular member or firm with services or products for sale. There is a tacit endorsement if, for instance, the person who teaches a class on wills and estates is an attorney at a local firm that wants church members to become clients for their wills and estate planning.

Like any other ministry in the church, dfree® must have complete integrity and not be used by people or companies who see our members as market share rather than people needing help. There are opportunities for a church or an affiliate of the church to enter into a strategic alliance with a firm and verify it with an explicit, written agreement reviewed by legal counsel. In such an instance, the church may have some interest in services or products for use by members that can benefit the church or affiliate. But the church will have to disclose the relationship to the congregation and make sure everyone involved knows as much about the alliance as possible. This can be a delicate, sensitive, and complicated area of endeavor. The simplest approach to this subject is to forbid anyone from using dfree® classes or events to sell any product without express written permission given by the church's leadership.

6. Be careful with people who are too far from being dfree®. Our church did benefit by having a dfree® chairman who was honest enough to admit that he wanted to become dfree®. But he was not having so much financial trouble that his circumstances represented a complete contradiction to the vision of the dfree® movement. If a person is really having tremendous financial problems, such as going through bankruptcy proceedings, being dragged into court for delinquent child support payments, or anything equally public and potentially embarrassing, they will not make effective leaders until they have resolved their problems.

7. Do not choose those who already have major responsibilities. The old adage is that if you want something done, ask someone who is already busy. But it is also true that some people are too busy to do a good job with an additional project. This is not a ministry that people should try to squeeze in between other ministries. This ministry requires laser-like focus and sustained dedication. dfree® does need church leaders involved but in a visibly supportive role more than an active leadership role.

Subcommittees

The dfree® committee is responsible for taking the dfree® vision and implementing the strategy that will motivate church members and community residents to access the resources being offered. The dfree® committee consists of the chairs and co-chairs of subcommittees that will assume responsibility for each category of work. Each subcommittee should have a chairperson and a co-chairperson to ensure that the work does not become the property or burden of one person and to provide for continuity if one person cannot serve as long as the other person. These subcommittees may include:

1. *dfree® Publicity and Promotion Committee:* This group is responsible for creating, distributing, and managing all dfree® communications. The primary job of this subcommittee is to make dfree® a household word among the target population. This may include website information, press releases, radio ads, flyers, and special announcements.

2. *dfree® Education Committee:* This committee is responsible for the educational component of dfree®. This is where people actually learn the content of the chosen curriculum, receive support from the instructors and others in

their classes, and track their progress. This committee must register people for classes, ensure that teachers are identified and trained, collect data from participants for tracking and evaluation, secure facilities for classes, and recommend people for dfree® milestone celebrations.

3. dfree® Sunday Committee: This committee is responsible for making sure dfree® Sunday has fresh and unique ideas that the pastor can include in the regular worship service. These additions to the services may be testimonials, award recognition, special skits, short video clips, guest speakers, and so on.

4. dfree® Capital Campaign Committee: This committee is responsible for making sure the church members remain aware of the capital/building needs of the church and that special appeals are continuously presented to the church. As the members become debt free, this committee works to help the church itself to remain debt free or become debt free.

5. dfree® Youth Committee: This committee is responsible for involving youth in dfree® activities and organizing youth-friendly events and classes for youth to understand the dfree® lifestyle before they ever get into debt or have any bills to pay.

6. dfree® Senior Committee: This committee is responsible for creating the part of the strategy that addresses and connects with the special financial needs of the elderly.

7. dfree® Partnerships Committee: The role of this committee is to identify and analyze potential partners for the church that can enhance its ability to conduct the dfree®

campaign. Many organizations, agencies, and businesses have an interest in financial literacy and other financial concerns addressed by dfree®. It can be helpful to have a committee that exclusively focuses on this part of the ministry.

If all these committees were in place and each committee had a chair and a co-chair, the dfree® committee would consist of 17 people: 14 committee chairs, a dfree® chair and co-chair, and the pastor as ex-officio. That makes a good, solid committee.

This group of chairs and co-chairs represent the dfree® committee — the executive leadership team that manages the dfree® efforts in the church. This leadership team, after getting a clear understanding of the pastor's vision, must do the following initial work:

- Establish measurable goals and priorities for the ministry.
- Develop a timetable for implementation.
- Recruit people to serve on the sub-committees.
- Create a budget for the dfree® campaign.
- Plan a schedule of meetings and conference calls.
- Plan a schedule of special dfree® events.
- Participate in group prayer for the work they are going to undertake.

People with certain skills and expertise make excellent candidates for dfree® leadership in a church. Not every church will have all of these professionals or skills within the congregation. In each instance organizations, institutions, and businesses in the church's community can supply volunteer support from people with the talent the church needs. Most banks will provide staff and materials for classes that teach the basics about banking and finance. Community colleges and universities are another great source of talent.

Even government agencies have information, staff, and other valuable resources to help churches and community organizations attempting to help people with their financial aptitude. Most of these institutions are thrilled to get the audience the church will create. Always remember, however, to protect church members from those who simply want to use the church to reach prospective customers for products and services the church may not support.

The following types of people can be very helpful with a dfree® campaign:

1. *Attorneys*: So many people receive threatening letters from creditors and others in the financial world that attorneys who are familiar with consumer laws can be helpful and resourceful.

2. *Financial professionals*: These include accountants, financial advisors, financial planners, tax specialists, real estate brokers, mortgage bankers, and investment bankers.

3. *Sales professionals*: Auto salespersons, consumer electronics salespersons, and real estate salespersons know and can explain the ins and outs of the retail industry.

4. *Business owners*: Entrepreneurs who have invested in themselves and are self-employed have flexible schedules and unique perspectives on finance.

5. *Educators:* These people have the skills to identify, adapt, and match curricula for appropriate audiences. They also have talent in presenting information in an organized and interesting way.

6. *Librarians:* These professionals, particularly reference librarians, specialize in information; their expertise about books, databases, and other materials related to business and finance can greatly assist individual and group efforts to learn these matters.

7. *Public relations professionals:* There are many more opportunities and strategies for reaching people with a message than the church bulletin. Sometimes even the language and the look of the church bulletin could use an injection of creativity. Public relations professionals can craft messages and implement ways to get the right message to the right people to get the right response.

8. *Graphic artists:* The artistic presentation of a dfree® activity can be more important than the words that describe it. A good graphic artist will give dfree® announcements and promotions an eye-catching and attractive look.

9. *Representatives of financial institutions:* These people will teach classes and help them understand products they may be considering as future options.

10. *Church officers and ministry leaders:* Leaders of the church should be visibly involved in many ways. They should not have so much responsibility that it detracts from their normal work as deacons, trustees, stewards, elder, deaconesses, clergy, and heads of ministries. But there is no substitute for the leaders of the church being involved in this ministry in a visible way.

11. *Great organizers:* These are people who just know how to get things done. They may have no particular financial expertise, but they can be trusted to get things happening and people participating.

12. *Dependable workers:* These folks are there on time, and they work without complaining. If they see a need, they don't wait to be asked to fill it. They are the glue that keeps things together. Every project needs some of them.

13. *Generous givers:* People who support the church love God and the church. They want what is best for the church, and they would like to see others support their church also. These people have been blessed and consider it a blessing to give. They will help the church help the members understand the blessing of financial peace and generosity better than anyone else.

14. *Youth:* Young people have innocent creativity and think "outside the box." They keep the work fresh and keep the others on their toes. And to be a part of this work is great training for their future endeavors. Besides, it takes young people to attract young people to the dfree® lifestyle. There is no better place for them besides leadership.

The dfree® team unity and its members' commitment will make or break the dfree® campaign. The pastor or leader can preach or teach on financial topics, make announcements, and offer periodic reminders that reinforce the ideas of paying bills as we go, paying bills on time, and living within our means. But it is going to take the sacrificial initiative of church or team members and others to really attack the culture of debt and help free people from the slavery that has them trapped financially. No one can do it alone, but everyone can do it together!

dfree®
Resources

PLEASE NOTE: This list of resources is representative and is by no means all-inclusive; dfree®, First Baptist Church, and Rev. DeForest Soaries Jr. cannot take responsibility for the content of the information shown or included with the resources on this list. Since, in particular, the Internet is an extremely dynamic process of gathering and sending information, we also cannot guarantee that online sources and resources will remain as stated here whenever users decide to access informational materials.

dfree®

www.mydfree.org — Updates and information about implementing dfree® as licensee and dfree® merchandise.

www.billiondollarpaydown.com — Set debt reduction goals, track and celebrate progress and form online groups to work together.

www.youtube.com/mydfree
www.facebook.com/mydfree
www.fbcsomerset.com — First Baptist Church of Lincoln
Gardens in Somerset, New Jersey.
www.dbsoaries.com

Websites

Money Management

www.mint.com — Money management tool.

money.strands.com — Free web-based financial management
tool kit.

www.schwabmoneywise.com — Money management education
and tools.

www.youneedabudget.com — Money management software.

www.quicken.com — Money management software.

General Information

www.irs.gov — Internal Revenue Service.

www.debtproofliving.com — Free newsletter daily "Everyday
Cheapskate" and other useful information.

www.kiplinger.com — Personal financial advice.

www.cuna.org — The Credit Union National Association
(CUNA), premier national trade association serving U.S. credit
unions.

www.daveramsey.com — Financial tools and information.

www.billeo.com — Personal online assistant.

Debt Reduction

www.freedomdebt.com — Debt negotiation service; fees charged.

www.jeanchatzky.com/debtdiet — The elimination strategy with tools; small annual fees.

www.powerpay.org — Debt elimination strategy with tools, including calculators.

Financial Literacy

www.mymoney.com — United States Treasury Department–sponsored basics about financial education.

www.360financialliteracy.org — Comprehensive financial literacy.

www.msgen.com — Helping kids get smart about money.

www.creativewealthintl.org — Financial literacy games and programs for children and students.

www.consumerjungle.org — Promotes consumer literacy among young adults.

www.financiallit.org — Financial literacy for adults.

www.moneyskill.org — Personal finance course for young adults.

fdic.gov/consumers/consumer/moneysmart/index.html — Money Smart, financial literacy sponsored by Federal Deposit Insurance Corporation; free curriculum available.

www.councilforeconed.org — Council for Economic Education, promotes economic and financial education in K–12 schools in the U.S. and internationally.

www.nefe.org — The National Endowment for Financial Education® (NEFE®), the only private, nonprofit national foundation dedicated to Americans' financial well-being.

www.practicalmoneyskills.com — Financial literacy information and tools for all ages.

Banking

www.fdic.gov — Federal Deposit Insurance Corporation.

www.federalreserve.gov — Federal Reserve.

www.icba.org — Independent Community Bankers of America.

www.bankjr.com — Understanding banks and banking.

Credit Cards

www.cardratings.com — For-profit organization devoted to educating consumers about credit cards.

www.bankrate.com/calculators/managing-debt/minimum-payment-calculator.aspx — Credit card payment calculator.

www.ftc.gov — Federal Trade Commission (FTC) deals with issues related to economic life in the U.S., the only federal agency with both consumer protection and competition jurisdiction in broad sectors of the economy.

Books

Bach, David. *The Finish Rich Workbook: Creating a Personalized Plan for a Richer Future.* New York: Broadway, 2003.

Berg, Jeff, and Jim Burgess. *The Debt-Free Church: Experiencing Financial Freedom While Growing Your Ministry.* Chicago: Moody Press, 1996.

Chatzky, Jean. *Pay It Down!: Debt-Free on $10 a Day.* New York: Portfolio, 2009.

Clark, Ken. *The Complete Idiot's Guide to Getting Out of Debt.* New York: Alpha, 2009.

Consumer Dummies. *Managing Your Money All-In-One for Dummies.* Hoboken, NJ: Wiley, 2008.

Covey, Stephen R. *The 7 Habits of Highly Effective People.* Philadelphia: Running, 2000.

Resources

Covey, Stephen R., A. Roger Merrill, and Rebecca R. Merrill. *First Things First: To Live, to Love, to Learn, to Leave a Legacy.* New York: Simon and Schuster, 1994.

Debtors Anonymous. *A Currency of Hope.* Needham, MA: Debtors Anonymous, 1999.

Fisher, Kenneth L. *The Ten Roads to Riches.* Hoboken, NJ: John Wiley & Sons, 2009.

Frankl, Viktor E. *Man's Search for Meaning: An Introduction to Logotherapy.* Boston: Beacon, 1959.

Garrett, Sheryl. *Personal Finance Workbook for Dummies.* Hoboken, NJ: Wiley, 2008.

Harris, Blaine, and Charles Coonradt. *The Four Laws of Debt Free Prosperity* (new edition: *The 4 Laws of Financial Prosperity*). Salt Lake City, UT: Franklin Covey/The Financial Wellness Group, 2009.

Hunt, Mary M. *Mary Hunt's Debt-Proof Living: The Complete Guide to Living Financially Free.* Nashville: Broadman & Holman, 1999.

Johnson, Stacy. *Life or Debt: A One-Week Plan for a Lifetime of Financial Freedom.* New York: Ballantine, 2002.

———. *Life or Debt 2010: A New Path to Financial Freedom.* New York: Pocket, 2010.

Khalifani-Cox, Lynnette. *Zero Debt: The Ultimate Guide to Financial Freedom.* 2nd Ed. South Orange: Advantage World Press, 2004.

Kiyosaki, Robert T. *Rich Dad, Poor Dad.* Paradise Valley, AZ: TechPress, 1998.

Manganiello, Anthony. *The Debt-Free Millionaire: Winning Strategies to Creating Great Credit and Retiring Rich.* Hoboken, NJ: John Wiley & Sons, 2009.

Mundis, Jerrold. *How to Get Out of Debt, Stay Out of Debt, and Live Prosperously (Based on the Proven Principles and Techniques of Debtors Anonymous).* New York: Bantam, 1988.

Osteen, Joel. *Your Best Life Now: 7 Steps to Living at Your Full Potential.* New York: Warner, 2004.

Ramsey, Dave. *The Total Money Makeover: A Proven Plan for Financial Fitness.* Nashville: Nelson, 2009.

Robbins, Anthony. *Unlimited Power.* New York: Simon and Schuster, 1997.

Roth, J. D. *Your Money: The Missing Manual.* Sebastopol, CA: O'Reilly, 2010.

Scatigna, Louis. *The Financial Physician: How to Cure Your Money Problems and Boost Your Financial Health.* Franklin Lakes, NJ: Career, 2010.

Schor, Juliet B. *The Overspent American: Why We Want What We Don't Need.* New York: Basic, 1998.

Schwartz, David Joseph. *The Magic of Thinking Big.* New York: Simon and Schuster, 1987.

Sethi, Ramit. *I Will Teach You to Be Rich.* New York: Workman, 2009.

Singletary, Michelle. *The 21-Day Financial Fast: Your Path to Financial Peace and Freedom.* Grand Rapids: Zondervan, 2014.

Sutton, Garrett. *The ABC's of Getting out of Debt: Turn Bad Debt into Good Debt and Bad Credit into Good Credit.* New York: Warner, 2004.

Tyson, Eric. *Personal Finance for Dummies.* Indianapolis: Wiley, 2010.

Vaz-Oxlade, Gail. *Debt-Free Forever: Take Control of Your Money and Your Life.* New York: Experiment, 2010.

Acknowledgments

This is my second book and one that I had almost given up on writing. I attribute its completion to a host of people who have been my "cloud of witnesses" cheering me on and praying for me as I have sought to share some of my experiences through writing. All of the names are too many to mention, but there are a few who deserve special thanks.

I begin by thanking God for allowing his precious treasure to be carried by this earthen vessel. I completely identify with the apostle Paul when he describes himself as the least of the apostles in 1 Corinthians 15:9. I have been blessed and honored to meet and affiliate with some of the finest pastors, leaders, and scholars in the world. I always feel as though I am the least of all of them. It is humbling to know that God would entrust me also with a portion of the work of building the kingdom of God. Only the power of Jesus' blood could have prepared me for this work. Thank God for Jesus!

I also owe a tremendous debt of thanks to my wife, Donna. She has been my chief critic and my number one cheerleader in this and all of my work. Donna is also the best Christian I know. Because of her example, our sons Malcolm and Martin have also been my prayer partners and supporters in this and all of my projects. My family made this book their project too.

Both of my parents were educators. Although my father is deceased, his grammar drills and example of excellence still guide me every day of my life and contributed significantly to my being able to communicate effectively, both verbally and in writing. My mother believes that I can do anything. Her confidence in me has given me more confidence in myself even when the words refused to flow.

My brother Dr. Craig Soaries and my sister, Attorney Terri Soaries, have been siblings and friends in all that I do, and this work has been no different. It is good to have siblings who earnestly pray for your success. My brother and sister-in-law, Alfred and Rochelle Pleasant, were praying also. They just did not know exactly what they were praying for because I did not tell them that I was writing a book.

My references to my early years in church refer to my having been raised in the Seventh Day Christian Church, an African American-led split from the Seventh-day Adventist denomination. The leaders of this denomination helped to raise me, and they gave me a chance to lead long before I was qualified or trained to do so. I am grateful for their biblical instruction, their nurturing, their generosity, and their faithfulness. I am who I am because of the foundation that I received in that movement.

My college and seminary professors did so much to prepare me for this ministry that words cannot describe my gratitude to them. Special thanks to Dr. Byron Shafer and Dr. Bart Collopy at Fordham University in New York City; Dr. Peter Paris,

Acknowledgments

Dr. Geddes Hanson, Dr. Randy Nichols, Dr. Gardner Taylor, and Dr. Clarice Martin at Princeton Theological Seminary; and Dr. Mary Olson, Dr. Len Sweet, Dr. Charles Booth, and Dr. Samuel DeWitt Proctor at United Theological Seminary in Dayton, Ohio. All of them poured knowledge into my inquiring mind and set high standards of intellectual excellence and integrity.

My first book was for teens, and I had the hardest time understanding where to aim my writing goals next. The economic crisis that so many families in our church and community face has become such a matter of urgency for us that I could not think about any other subject. And so many churches have asked for help with a strategy for their members to address their finances that I could hear God calling me to put our experience and strategy in writing. After years of waiting, Zondervan accepted my manuscript for this book enthusiastically and committed to this book in ways that are humbling. The leaders at Zondervan — Moe Girkins, Stan Gundry, Sandra Vander Zicht, Don Gates, Robin Geelhoed — have all contributed to making this process a pleasure. Dr. Dudley Delffs helped me make this work relevant to a much broader audience than I had originally intended.

But I am also indebted to Dr. C. Jeffrey Wright and the leadership team at Urban Ministries Inc. (UMI) for their vision and commitment to this project. Dr. Wright pushed me toward completion based upon his knowledge of needs in African American churches and his commitment to meeting those needs. UMI began promoting the book verbally before they even saw the outline. Their faith and courage forced me to expand my faith, change my schedule, and finish the book.

Acknowledgments

The most important contribution Dr. Wright made to my process was to add Mary Lewis as my editor and coach. What a talented, integral, focused, professional, and brilliant human being. It would have taken me twenty years to write this book had it not been for Mary Lewis. What a blessing she has been.

Both Lisa Pickrum and Soledad O'Brien really expanded my own understanding about the broad significance of our work with dfree®. They both helped me to realize that what we're doing had implications far beyond our church and that we should get the message to as many people as we can. Ms. Pickrum convinced me that dfree® was really a big deal and not just a local church project. When Ms. O'Brien and CNN decided to focus on First Baptist Church of Lincoln Gardens in their documentary "Almighty Debt," it was exposure that I had never dreamed my work would receive. These two women motivated me to take our work to the next level.

My pastor friends who write books have been great inspirations and encouragement. Dr. Timothy Winters, Dr. William Watley, Dr. Donald Hilliard Jr., Dr. Marvin McMickle, Dr. Jesse Mapson, Dr. Gerald Lamont Thomas, Dr. Cynthia Hale, Dr. H. Beecher Hicks Jr., and Dr. Floyd Flake were my inspirations whose accomplishments convinced me that it is possible to be a pastor and a writer.

Finally, my church family at First Baptist Church of Lincoln Gardens in Somerset, New Jersey, has been nothing less than 100 percent supportive of this project. For five years they helped create the dfree® strategy that became the subject matter of this project. They have been praying for my book writing, at my request, for two years. Charles Corpening was the first church member to support the dfree® vision and our first dfree® teacher, and Kwabena Yamoah was our first dfree® coordinator. Without First Baptist, this would all be theory. Thank God for a great church.

Finally, I thank God for the plan of salvation and for loving me enough to give me a chance to become a "new creation" (2 Corinthians 5:17).

DeForest B. Soaries Jr.
November 11, 2010

I have Zondervan to thank for the opportunity to update *dfree®: Breaking Free from Financial Slavery* with new insights and data. Unfortunately, millions of people are stuck in financial circumstances without a strategy to improve their situations. However, many people are finding that it is completely possible to transform their finances by using our dfree® strategy and content. Today hundreds of churches are part of the dfree® movement and volunteers are using the word of God and the power of God to help set financial captives free. Thanks to the Christian community for embracing our message and approach to financial freedom.

Thanks to the team at Zondervan, led by Stan Gundry and Sandy Vander Zicht, for helping the dfree® movement with this second edition. And special thanks to my dfree® leadership team for their tireless work with churches everywhere: Joy Gardner, Keri Spencer, Willie Mae Veasey, Dan Veasey, Sonaya Williams, Tamika Stembridge, Ivel Turner, Michelle Dutton, Brianna Smallwood, Martin Soaries, Malcolm Soaries, Jonnice Slaughter, Kelli Webster and Mike Pinnix. Special thanks to Bob Johnson and Stacey Edmonds for producing the "dfree® to be Free" TV show used with our dfree® classes and seen by thousands of people.

I thank God every day for the best church on the world – First Baptist Church of Lincoln Gardens. The publication of this book marks my 25th anniversary as the senior pastor of this marvelous community.

Of course none of my work would be possible without the unconditional love and support of my wife of thirty-years, Donna. No one should attempt to do what I did without having a partner like my wife. Thank you, Donna, for making me better than I would be without you.

I thank God for delivering me from the bondage I was in. I pray that my testimony will be a blessing to you as you "Say Yes to No Debt."

DeForest B. Soaries, Jr.
February 2015